HISTORY OF INHERITANCE LAW

Everything You Need to Know

Harry L. Munsinger, J.D., Ph.D.

Copyright © 2020 Harry L. Munsinger, J.D., Ph.D.

All rights reserved. No part of this book may be used or reproduced by any means, graphic, electronic, or mechanical, including photocopying, recording, taping or by any information storage retrieval system without the written permission of the author except in the case of brief quotations embodied in critical articles and reviews.

Archway Publishing books may be ordered through booksellers or by contacting:

Archway Publishing
1663 Liberty Drive
Bloomington, IN 47403
www.archwaypublishing.com
844-669-3957

Because of the dynamic nature of the Internet, any web addresses or links contained in this book may have changed since publication and may no longer be valid. The views expressed in this work are solely those of the author and do not necessarily reflect the views of the publisher, and the publisher hereby disclaims any responsibility for them.

Any people depicted in stock imagery provided by Getty Images are models, and such images are being used for illustrative purposes only. Certain stock imagery © Getty Images.

ISBN: 978-1-4808-9841-7 (sc)
ISBN: 978-1-4808-9842-4 (e)

Library of Congress Control Number: 2020921318

Print information available on the last page.

Archway Publishing rev. date: 11/04/2020

CONTENTS

Introduction vii

Chapter 1	Origins of Inheritance Law	1
Chapter 2	English Inheritance Law	18
Chapter 3	American Inheritance Law	36
Chapter 4	Probate and Will Contests	53
Chapter 5	Origin of Trusts and Fiduciary Duties	69
Chapter 6	Wills of Famous People	86
Chapter 7	Infamous Will Disputes	103
Chapter 8	Notorious Business Trusts	119

Conclusions 135
Endnotes 151

INTRODUCTION

You can't take it with you, so what happens to your assets when you die? People generally want to pass their wealth to a surviving spouse and children—but how can they do that? Must they draft a will or trust to pass assets to the next generations, or will the courts automatically distribute their assets for them? The answer is you can pass assets to your spouse and children by drafting a will or trust, or by letting a probate court administer your estate through intestate succession—although intestate succession may be different from what you intend. When a person dies without a will or trust, distribution of his or her property is governed by the estate code where the individual lived. If you don't feel comfortable allowing a probate court determine who takes your property, then draft a will or trust expressing your personal intent.[1] It's good practice to draft a will or trust to control the distribution of your estate if you own significant assets and you want to make certain the property goes to the persons you love. Estate codes treat all families alike and may not distribute your assets to those you love.

Historically, laws of succession were written to benefit powerful interest groups, but in America, inheritance is a significant source of savings for many.

Purpose of Inheritance Laws

Inheritance is a major source of wealth for many Americans. Experts estimate that around 80 percent of American household wealth was inherited rather than earned. Studies indicate that Americans who died in 2015 left around $177,000 to their heirs.[2] That amount of inherited wealth can help a family buy a new home, pay for children's education, or supplement retirement savings.

Originally, the laws of succession were shaped and controlled by wealthy groups for their own benefit. For example, early English laws of succession were developed to protect the interests of kings and wealthy aristocrats who owned large estates in feudal tenure. English common law and feudal tenure produced the doctrine of primogeniture—the inheritance of titles and all family real estate by the eldest surviving son. This system of inheritance ensured that wealthy English families would continue to own large estates for generations.[3] In contrast, the American colonies developed democratic laws of inheritance designed to meet the needs of families who owned small farms. Most colonial fathers passed the family farm to their sons in equal shares.

Land was cheap and plentiful in America, and few families who owned large plantations in the colonies, so American laws of succession favored distributing wealth equally to all members of a family rather than giving everything to the eldest son. The family farm was usually divided among the surviving spouse and children when the husband/father died. If an inherited farm proved too small to support a family, there was plenty of land waiting to be purchased, improved, or homesteaded on the western frontier for anyone ambitious enough to move and improve the land. Most colonial Americans were not concerned with keeping large land holdings intact by passing the entire farm to the eldest son; in America, anyone with ambition could acquire a farm of his own with hard work because there was so much cheap land available.

A somewhat different inheritance system developed in some southern colonies because tobacco and cotton were grown by slaves on large plantations.

The laws of succession in a few southern colonies developed along lines similar to English inheritance laws because aristocratic plantation owners wanted to pass everything to their firstborn son and keep the family plantation intact.[4] Today, Americans who own significant assets generally draft wills or trusts to control the inheritance of their property and distribute their assets equitably among the surviving spouse and children.

To understand how your assets are distributed when you die, you need to know about wills, trusts, probate, estate administration, and intestate succession.

A Will

Black's Law Dictionary defines a will as "an instrument by which a person makes a disposition of his real and personal property, to take effect after his death, and which by its own nature is ambulatory and revocable during his lifetime."[5] A will must be in writing, be signed and dated by the testator before a notary and at least two witnesses, name an executor, beneficiaries, and describe the disposition of the estate. Ambulatory means the will is subject to modification during the testator's lifetime.

A Trust

Black's Law Dictionary defines a trust as "a legal entity created by a grantor for the benefit of designated beneficiaries under the laws of the state and the valid trust instrument. The trustee holds a fiduciary responsibility to manage the trust's corpus assets and income for the economic benefit of all of the beneficiaries."[6] A trust must be in writing, be signed and dated by the grantor and trustee, and name beneficiaries. The terms of the trust govern how the assets are administered and distributed. The trustee holds legal title to trust property for the economic use and benefit of others and owes a fiduciary duty to manage the trust for the beneficiaries.

Probate.

Black's Law Dictionary defines probate as a "court procedure by which a will is proved to be valid or invalid; though in current usage this term has been expanded to generally refer to the legal process wherein the estate of a decedent is administered."[7] When a person dies, the original will must be submitted to a probate court to determine whether it's valid and to allow the court to appoint an administrator for the estate. The American probate process was borrowed from English common law, which followed ancient Roman practices governing the handling of wills. Probate is a procedure for proving the validity of a will, legal rules for administering the estate according to the terms of the will, proper steps for closing the estate administration once all the assets have been collected, debts paid and the assets distributed to beneficiaries according to the terms of the will, or a determination of heirs if there is no will.

Estate Administration

The will or a probate judge names an executor to administer the estate—either independently without court supervision or under the watchful eye of a probate court. The executor collects the decedent's assets, drafts an inventory and appraisement, pays legitimate claims, files required tax returns, sells property to raise funds, and distributes assets to the proper beneficiaries. After the estate administration is complete, the executor files a final inventory and appraisement with the probate court and closes the estate. To protect beneficiaries, some states require that each step in the administration of an estate be approved by a probate court. Other states allow an independent administration of the estate without court oversight, which is a simpler and cheaper way to probate a will—although it runs the modest risk that an executor might defraud the beneficiaries by distributing assets improperly. What happens to your property if you don't leave a will or trust?

Intestate Succession

If you don't leave a will or trust when you die, your assets are distributed according to the laws of intestate succession. Your heirs are determined by the estate code where you resided before you died.

For example, if you die in Texas without a valid will, how your estate is distributed depends on whether the decedent was married, whether the property is community or separate, whether an asset is real estate or personal property, whether the decedent was single or widowed, and whether he or she left surviving children.[8]

Married with Children—Separate Property

When a decedent was married and left a surviving spouse and children, the spouse receives a life estate in any separate property real estate the person owned at the time of death; this means the surviving spouse may occupy the property as long as he or she is living but can't sell the separate property real estate. The children take their parent's separate property real estate in equal shares when the surviving parent dies. Separate personal property of a deceased married person with children is divided two-thirds (in equal shares) to the children and one-third to the surviving spouse.

Married with Children—Community Property

When a married deceased person left a surviving spouse and children of both parties, the surviving spouse takes all the community property (both real and personal property) when the spouse dies. However, if there are children from outside the existing marriage, then the children take one-half the community real estate and one-half the community personal property in equal shares. The surviving spouse takes the remaining half of the community real estate and community personal property.

Single or Widowed without Children

If a person dies and was single or widowed without children, the heirs depend on who survives the decedent. If only his parents survive, they take all his or her real and personal property in equal shares.

However, if both parents and siblings survive, then one-half the real and personal property goes to the parents in equal shares, and one-half goes to the siblings in equal shares.

Widowed with Children

If a widow or widower dies without a will, his or her property passes to the children in equal shares.

Married without Children

If a married person dies without children, who takes his or her property depends on which family members are surviving. For example, if the parents survive, one-quarter of all separate real estate goes to the mother, one-quarter of all separate real estate goes to the father of the decedent, and the remaining one-half of the separate real property goes to the surviving spouse. If there is no surviving parent, then one-half of the separate real property goes to the decedent's surviving siblings or their descendants, and one-half goes to the surviving spouse. If only one parent survives the decedent, one-quarter of the separate real estate goes to the surviving parent, one-quarter goes to surviving siblings or their descendants, and one-half goes to the surviving spouse. If no parents or siblings of the deceased survive, all the separate real estate goes to the surviving spouse. If no siblings of the deceased survive him or her, then one-half the separate real estate goes to the surviving parents, and one-half goes to the surviving spouse. All the other property (separate assets other than real property and all community property) goes to the surviving spouse.

The Texas Estate Code was designed to be fair to family members, but it treats all families alike no matter their circumstances, so intestate succession may not be the best alternative to a valid will that expresses the decedent's unique preferences about who should take his or her separate and community property at death. It's generally better to leave a will or trust when you die if you own significant assets so you will be certain your loved ones receive the benefits of your estate according to your wishes.

In addition to a will, several other documents constitute a basic estate plan.

Basic Estate Plan

If you have assets you want to leave to specific individuals, or if you have moved to a new state, recently married, had a baby, retired, been divorced, or experienced any significant life change, you should put your financial house in order by talking to an estate attorney who can draft a basic estate plan to meet your unique needs. The basic elements of an estate plan include a will, power of attorney, medical power of attorney, directive to physicians, a HIPAA release, and a living trust if you want to avoid the expense and publicity of probate or have minor children or disabled family members who need care, guidance, and support.[9]

Anyone with significant assets should have a basic estate plan to make certain their wealth is distributed to those they love and the proper persons are appointed to make health and financial decisions concerning end of life situations. A will determines how assets are distributed to adults or into a trust for the protection of children or disabled individuals. A general power of attorney grants another adult the authority to act for you if you are unable to handle your own personal or financial affairs. A medical power of attorney gives another adult authority to make health-care decisions for you when a physician certifies you are unable to make those decisions yourself. A directive to physicians communicates your wishes about end-of-life care. Finally, a HIPAA release authorizes the disclosure of confidential health information to listed individuals.

Some families draft a living trust to handle their unique estate needs and avoid the expense and publicity of probate.

A living trust gives privacy and control over assets after a person dies. Trusts avoid the publicity associated with probate, and a trustee will manage and distribute the estate according to the terms of the trust document for the health, maintenance, support, or education of a surviving spouse and children who may need financial protection and guidance. A trust is also helpful if any family members are disabled and cannot care for themselves.

For larger estates that contain substantial assets, families often establish a limited partnership using trusts to control and manage the assets. A limited partnership allows central control of a farm, business, or investment portfolio and lets family members hold minority interests in the family farm, business, or investment portfolio. A family limited partnership may also offer a marketability or lack of control discount that can lower or eliminate expensive estate taxes at the death of an older family member. In addition, the family limited partnership places another layer of security and legal protection between your assets and potential creditors.

A will can be changed at any time by drafting a new one or adding a codicil to an existing will. If there is no will, state intestate laws control who takes your assets according to the current estate code where you lived before your death. Wills and trusts have served numerous purposes over the centuries in England and America, but they have ancient origins in the early legal systems of Mesopotamia, Greece, Rome, and England.

Origins of Inheritance Law

Many of our modern laws of succession have ancient roots in the Code of Hammurabi, which contained several early rules about inheritance. Greeks introduced the use of wills to transfer land when the father died and there was no surviving son. The Romans borrowed ideas about succession from the Greeks and formalized them in the Twelve Tables, which listed the rights and duties of every Roman citizen, including laws of inheritance. In early Anglo-Saxon law, the will was an important document that could dispose of personal property and prove the ownership of land after the owner died. In modern times, with the development of recorded deeds and land-title records, the ownership of assets can be proved independent of a will. Other modern instruments, such as a living trust, tenancy in common with right of survivorship, or a pay on death bank account (often called a Totten trust) can be substituted for a will. The most important alternative to a will is the living trust, which can hold and distribute assets during the life of an individual and transfer ownership at death to named beneficiaries without the need for probate.

An alternative to drafting a will or trust is giving away money while you are living.

Lifetime Gifts

Now that Americans are living longer and have a guaranteed income from Social Security, lifetime gifts are becoming a more important source of generational wealth transfer. Also, because the exemption from estate tax for lifetime gifts in 2020 was $11.58 million for every American, fewer families are concerned about avoiding estate taxes.[10] Grandparents may choose to pay college expenses for their grandchildren or help their children buy a home during their lifetimes rather than waiting until death to transfer assets to their children. However, wills and trusts are still important to individuals who want to make certain their assets pass to the proper persons. Also, many older individuals worry that they may run out of money before they die, so they retain assets rather than spending all their money or giving it to their children during their lifetime.

Only living individuals or corporations can own assets, so when a person dies, there must be rules determining who takes the dead person's assets. There are several possible sets of rules that could be used. The state could confiscate the dead person's assets, statutes could be passed to control who inherits wealth when a person dies, or the distribution of assets can be left to the discretion of the individual who owns the property. English and American inheritance laws include elements of all three systems. The government takes a portion of a wealthy person's assets when the person dies in the form of estate taxes levied when assets are transferred at death. If there are no known heirs, all a decedent's assets pass to the state. Laws of intestate succession govern the distribution of property when a person dies without a will, and any competent adult can draft a will or trust stating how he or she wants property distributed at death.

What are the general rules of intestate succession?

Intestate Succession

Intestate laws generally distribute a decedent's assets to the surviving spouse and children or grandchildren if there is no will or trust. If there is no surviving spouse or descendants, then surviving parents or siblings usually take the decedent's property. If there is no surviving parent or sibling, then other more distant relatives will inherit the estate. In early English history, the inheritance of land and the inheritance of personal property were handled by different court systems. Today, the inheritance of land and personal property is controlled by a single unified system of inheritance law in England or America, and a surviving spouse generally takes a larger share of the decedent's estate than in earlier generations. In early English law, after the Norman Conquest, primogeniture was the common way to dispose of real property held in feudal tenure, which meant all titles, the land, and income from the land passed to the eldest surviving son. Daughters received a portion of the decedent's personal property and were married to other aristocratic sons through arranged marriage contracts negotiated by the parents. Younger sons received a small portion of the decedent's personal property and were expected to enter the military or clergy to earn a living.

Origins of Primogeniture

The English doctrine of primogeniture developed after the introduction of feudalism by King William following the Norman

Conquest of 1066.[11] For centuries after the conquest, title to English land was held in feudal tenure, which meant real estate could not be sold but instead had to be transferred to the eldest surviving son. This system ensured that large feudal estates remained in the same family for generations rather than being divided among a decedent's sons. Under primogeniture, the eldest surviving son inherited all his father's land and his title, and daughters and younger sons inherited portions of the father's personal property. Daughters were married to wealthy sons of aristocratic families, and younger sons went into the clergy or military.

The English system of primogeniture was introduced by King William to perpetuate the control of large feudal estates by friendly lords and retain political power in the hands of England's Norman aristocrats by concentrating ownership and control of land among loyal nobles. Primogeniture meant that large landholdings were not broken up and distributed to several sons in each succeeding generation, enabling Norman lords to support troops to fight for their king when called to arms. Personal property, on the other hand, was divided among the decedent's surviving children in Norman England. Land and the income from land were far more important than personal property for the maintenance of power in ancient England, and it passed to the eldest surviving son under the doctrine of primogeniture.

A different system of inheritance developed in the American colonies because feudal tenure was not viable in America and land was abundant, and for centuries, the English king didn't worry about colonial rebellion. Because there was ample cheap land on the frontier in America, capitalism developed rather than feudal tenure, except among some southern colonies where large plantation owners used slaves to grow cotton and tobacco.

Among the North American colonies, sons inherited equal shares of the family farm when parents died, although in some colonies the oldest son inherited a double share, perhaps a legacy of early biblical traditions. Among America's southern colonies, a form of primogeniture evolved and lasted until the American Civil War, because large plantations based on slavery and the growing of tobacco or cotton were often passed to the eldest surviving son.[12] The inheritance laws of southern American colonies and the southern states prior to the Civil War were designed to keep large tobacco and cotton plantations intact because aristocratic families wanted to perpetuate a landed gentry supported by slave labor. This entire economic system of large plantations, slave labor, and the inheritance laws supporting it was swept away by the American Civil War.

Wills and trusts have a long and complex history. The next chapter will examine the ancient origin of our inheritance laws.

CHAPTER 1

Origins of Inheritance Law

The laws of succession are shaped by competition for political power, social influence, personal safety, and money. Inheritance laws have several purposes and offer various ways to pass land, titles, and personal property to the next generation in an orderly manner. Important goals of early inheritance laws were to keep ancestral land within the family, maintain large estates within aristocratic families, and pass family assets to surviving spouses and children. Many basic concepts of inheritance law were first developed in an organized way during the reign of King Hammurabi and published around 1780 BC in Mesopotamia.[13] These early laws of succession were adopted, modified, and expanded by Greek, Roman, Jewish, French, and English peoples over the centuries. American inheritance laws derive primarily from English common law, but developed differently after the American Revolution.

Most legal historians trace the origins of our current laws of inheritance to the Code of Hammurabi.

The Code of Hammurabi

King Hammurabi ruled Babylon from 1792 BC to 1750 BC, and his code is believed to have been written and published around 1780

BC. Although there were earlier legal systems that included rules of inheritance, the Code of Hammurabi covered many important topics of succession and is considered by many historians to mark the beginnings of modern inheritance law. The Code of Hammurabi is most famous for its harsh system of retributive justice ("an eye for an eye"), but the code also contained early elements of civil procedures, contracts, family law, criminal law, and rules of inheritance.

Babylonian society contained three social classes and a king who ruled everyone: the highest social class consisted of large landowners, merchants, priests, and government officials; in the middle were artisans, shopkeepers, teachers, small farmers, and laborers; and, at the bottom of society were slaves bought at market or captured in battle. King Hammurabi stood above these social classes and was not subject to his own laws because he could revise them at any time. When the Magna Carta was signed on June 15, 1215, at Runnymede, England, a king accepted for the first time restrictions on his absolute power to write laws and govern as he pleased. Americans owe many of their civil liberties to that ancient English document.

The Hammurabi Code applied equally to all classes of society except the king, and it contained laws covering criminal justice, families, contracts, torts (harm caused by negligence), and laws of inheritance. We discuss only the laws of succession in this chapter.

Guardianship

The Hammurabi Code provided guardianship and care for minor children after the death of their father. For example, law 29 stated that if a son was too young to conduct his father's business, the judges would give one-third of the fields and garden to his mother, and she would raise him to adulthood. The code also allowed a man to deed property to a wife or daughter during his lifetime. Moreover, the code protected a widow's gifted property from her children if they disputed her title after the father died. Law 150 said that if a man gave his wife a field, garden, house, or goods and delivered a sealed deed to her, then after his death, her children could not make a claim for that property—it belonged to the widow. Law 150 also allowed a widow to leave property to her children but not to her brother—presumably to keep the land within the husband's family. The code also gave some rights to Mesopotamian women.

Widows Inheritance Rights

The Code of Hammurabi contained provisions affecting women, including the distribution of a wife's dowry at her death. Law 162 stated that if a man took a wife, she bore him children, and that woman died, her dowry belonged to her children rather than the surviving husband. The code also dealt with how children of two different mothers would inherit property from their mothers and father. Law 167 said that if a man took a wife, she bore him children, that woman died, the man took another wife, she bore him children, and later the father died, then the children should not share equally in the entire estate but would instead inherit the dowries of their respective mothers and divide equally the goods of their father.

Sons received generous inheritance rights under the Hammurabi Code.

Son's Inheritance Rights

The code contained several provisions concerning the inheritance rights of sons. It specifically prohibited a father from disinheriting a son except for good cause and discouraged disinheritance even if the son deserved it by giving him a chance to reform. Law 168 stated that if a man intended to disinherit his son, the judge must determine the facts of the case, and if the son does not deserve the heavy penalty of disinheritance, the father may not disinherit him. This law implies that sons had a legal right to inherit property from their fathers and that the right to inherit could not be negated except for good cause shown before a court. Law 169 said that even if a son deserved to be disinherited, the judge should consider a pardon for the son's first offense against his father and allow the father to disinherit his son only after a second offense.

Illegitimate Children

The Hammurabi Code also dealt with the inheritance rights of illegitimate children. Law 170 stated that if a man had children by his wife and his maid servant and called the maid's children "my children," they should share equally in the father's goods after he died, although the wife's children got first choice of their father's assets. In contrast, law 171 said that if a man did not call the maid's offspring "my children," they would take nothing at their father's death. But the maid and her children should be set free at the death of the father. The wife would receive her dowry and the gifts her husband deeded on a tablet, and she could dwell in her husband's house and enjoy his property so long as she lived, but she could not sell the house or other property of her husband because it belonged to her children.

The Hammurabi Code also discussed the case where a husband gave nothing to his widow, and their children tried to drive her from the home. Under these conditions, a widow could petition the court for protection. Law 172 said that if a widow did not receive a gift when her husband died, she could keep her dowry, receive the goods of her husband's house in a portion similar to that of a son, and live in the house until she died. If the children tried to drive her out of the house, a judge would inquire whether the children were in the wrong, and if they were, she would be allowed to stay in the home so long as she lived.

Inheritance of a Dowry

The code dealt with inheritance rules when a widow remarried and had children with both men. Law 173 stated that if a woman should bear children of a second husband, all her children shall divide her dowry equally. On the other hand, law 174 says if she has no children by a second husband, her first children shall receive all her dowry in equal shares. The code also set up a trust for a widow if she remarried. Law 177 stated if a widow remarried, the judge would entrust the former husband's estate to the second husband for the benefit of the mother and her minor children. The trustee husband was not authorized to sell the mother's estate, but if he did, the buyer had to give the purchase money to the mother and her children rather than to the second husband. The trust had to be in writing, and the new husband was required to administer the estate and raise the minor children but was not authorized to sell the children's estate while they lived. If the second husband sold the estate anyway, he had to forfeit the money received to the mother's sons rather than being allowed to keep it, but the buyer could keep the estate he had purchased.

The code also protected daughters and instructed judges to give them a dowry if their father gave them nothing when he died. Law 180 said if a father did not give a dowry to his daughter, she would receive, as her share of the father's estate, the portion of a son for her life. After her death, her portion would pass to her brothers.

The Code of Hammurabi contained important elements of modern inheritance law, such as providing for the care of minor children after the death of their father, allowing a husband to deed property to his wife and daughter prior to his death, and protecting a widow's children by requiring that her dowry pass to them when she died. The code also dealt with how children of two different mothers would inherit their dowries. It prohibited a father from disinheriting his son except for good cause and even discouraged disinheritance if the son deserved it by giving him a chance to reform. Illegitimate children were protected and allowed to receive a portion of their father's estate, but only if their father called them "my children," making them legitimate. The code also proscribed what to do when a husband gave nothing to his widow or when a widow remarried and had children with another man. A remarkable beginning to inheritance law despite its harsh basic principle of retributive justice (an eye for an eye).

The next developments in inheritance law occurred among the ancient city-states of Greece.

Greek Inheritance Laws

Historians believe Greeks were the first to use written wills to control the distribution of an estate after a person died. However, a Greek will only became effective if there was no surviving natural born son of the decedent.[14] In ancient Athens, legitimate male citizens over twenty years of age could draft a will. When adopted Greek males died without children, their assets were inherited by the family of the person(s) who adopted them. Greek males could will assets to unrelated persons if they had no sons. On the other hand, slaves and foreigners had their property confiscated by the Greek city-state when they died.

Anyone with a male heir in Athens could not draft a valid will because his property automatically passed by law to his son(s) when he died. If an Athenian male had only daughters, he could name an unrelated male in his will as his heir, but that male was obligated to marry one of the decedent's daughters if he wanted to keep the inheritance. An Athenian male had to be competent to draft a will—he could not suffer from a mental or physical disease that would render him incapable of making a will. Greek law required that a will be signed by several witnesses to attest its authenticity and then given to an administrator to implement after the testator died. If a Greek male was in prison or held captive, he could not draft a valid will because it was assumed the terms of the will had been dictated by his captors. Ancient Greek wills could be announced orally before several witnesses, but most Greeks preferred to put their wills in writing so there was less uncertainty about the terms. Greek inheritance laws controlled the distribution of an estate if the decedent left surviving sons.

Greek Sons Inherited Equally

Greek inheritance laws generally gave sons equal shares of their father's estate, which meant that few ancient Greek families were able to maintain large land holdings for generations (unlike later English aristocrats, who practiced primogeniture). English aristocratic families retained large land holdings in a single family for generations because the land and title passed to the eldest surviving son; under Greek inheritance laws, that didn't happen. Greek land was divided among all the sons, so the family land was partitioned into smaller and smaller parcels over succeeding generations. If there was only one son, this system didn't dissipate family land during that generation, but if a father left several sons, his property would be partitioned into many smaller parcels, until after a few generations each son received only a few acres of land. This Greek inheritance system meant that sons eventually had little land to pass along, unless they increased their holdings themselves.

Aristotle was one of the first to point out the dangers of dividing land among several sons and argued that the practice produced poverty and social strife because after a few generations, each son received too small a parcel of land to support a family. If a Greek father died without leaving descendants, the land passed to his relatives, concentrating property in fewer households and creating a few wealthy Greek families. This concentration of land in a few families happened during plagues or wars when many sons died. During those trying times, land could be consolidated and large parcels accumulated within a single Greek family if the members were diligent, prudent, and hardworking.

If a Greek male had children, his estate passed according to the Greek laws of intestate succession even if he left a will.

Greek Intestate Succession

Ancient Greek inheritance laws differed among the various city-states. Greek laws of inheritance were codified in the fifth century BC in the Gortyn Code.[15] The code dealt with disputed ownership of slaves, rape, adultery, how to bring a suit, divorce, marriage, property rights, and inheritance law. Greek males managed the family property, although a wife's property was often held in separate title. If a wife died, her husband became the manager of her property in trust for their children. The father could not sell the widow's entrusted land without the children's permission. If the husband remarried, the widow's children immediately received title to their mother's property so it could not be sold. If a Greek wife died without leaving descendants, her property reverted to her closest male relatives rather than passing to her surviving husband so the land would remain in her family. If a Greek husband died and left minor children, the wife managed his property in trust for their children until they were adults. However, if the Greek children were adults when their father died, his property was immediately divided among the adult children, with the land going to his sons and personal property to the daughters.

Adopted Greek children were entitled to the same inheritance rights as natural children. Greek widows who received no property as a gift, dowry, or inheritance from their dead husbands could obtain their proper share of the estate by going to court and filing suit—an early example of women having some legal protection of their property rights. If a Greek father died without sons, his daughter inherited his estate, but she was required to marry one of her father's close male relatives to keep the land within his family. This situation created what was called an Epikleros—a Greek woman who inherited her father's estate.

Epikleros

A Greek daughter who inherited her father's property if he left no sons was called an Epikleros.[16] Greek women were generally not allowed to hold property in their own name (except Spartan women, who could own land even if they were not married), but if the family had no sons, then the eldest daughter took the land. However, to keep the land in her father's family, the eldest daughter was required to marry her father's nearest relative, who would hold title to the land and pass it on to their descendants. If the eldest daughter was already married, she had to divorce her husband and marry her father's nearest relative, beginning with her father's brother if he survived and moving to more distant relatives of her father to find a surviving relative and keep the land in her father's family. It did not matter whether or not the daughter's mother was living—the eldest daughter inherited the land and had to marry a near male relative of her father if there were no sons born to the family. The probability that all three children in a family will be female is approximately twenty-five percent. [17]We turn next to Roman inheritance laws, which borrowed several basic ideas of succession from the Greeks and refined them into one of the most coherent legal codes of the ancient world.

Roman Inheritance Laws

The best preserved Roman legal text is the Law of the Twelve Tables, dating from the fifth century BC.[18] These laws were drafted to make Roman justice uniform and limit judges applying different rules to similar legal situations. The Twelve Tables didn't provide a complete set of rules covering all areas of modern law, but they were a major improvement over earlier Roman practice. The Tables covered contract law, civil procedures, family relationships, and Roman rules of inheritance.

Roman Fathers and Sons

Roman fathers held enormous power over their children. For example, Law I from Table IV gave fathers the power of life and death over a son born of a lawful marriage. Fathers and sons were considered a single person under Roman law, so when the father died, his son immediately succeeded to ownership of the father's estate and all other rights and duties accumulated by the father during his lifetime, including any titles the father held. The son had been a joint owner of the father's property and titles while his father lived, and when the father died, the son automatically owned the land and any titles by right of survivorship. If a Roman father had no natural born sons, he could name an heir in his will.

Law IV of Table IV said when a woman brings forth a son within ten months of the death of her husband, the baby is considered a legitimate son of the dead father and shall be a legal heir of his father's estate. Under modern law, the interval after the death of a father when a newborn is considered legitimate varies from 280 days in English common law to 300 days in the France civil code (average gestation for humans is 280 days). Roman law had special rules for inheritance when a decedent left no will.

Roman Intestate Succession

Law II of Table V said when a father died intestate (without a will) and left no proper heir, his nearest agnate (a person descended from the same male ancestor) would be his heir. Law III of Table V stated that when a freedman (a slave who had purchased or was given his freedom) died intestate and his patron survived him, the freedman's estate would be given to his patron. Law V of Table V held that when co-heirs wanted to divide their shares of an estate, three arbiters would be appointed who would give each beneficiary his proper part of the estate. Law VI of Table V said that when a head of household died intestate and left a proper heir who had not reached the age of maturity, the deceased father's nearest agnate would be appointed as guardian of the estate until the son was an adult.

Ancient Romans often drafted wills to distribute their assets following death, especially if they were wealthy or important government officials.

The Roman Will

The ancient Romans borrowed laws governing the drafting of wills from the Greeks and made refinements that are still used in modern estate planning.[19] Originally, Roman wills were publicly announced before seven witnesses so they knew the testator's intent. Once announced, a Roman will could not be changed—instead, a new will had to be announced before witnesses if the testator wanted to change who would receive his property or if he acquired new assets. Romans soon learned that trusting the memory of living witnesses was not always satisfactory, so their wills were written, signed, and sealed by witnesses. The earliest Roman wills were made by legionnaires on the eve of battle, and they were usually oral. Roman wills could be oral or written but were usually in writing and attested by seven witnesses.

Roman patricians had their wills published as legislation by the Senate, whereas common Roman citizens used informal wills that were sufficient to transfer modest amounts of property. However, a Roman citizen could not appoint an heir outside his bloodline through an informal will. If he wanted to leave property to someone outside his family, the will needed to be formal, in writing, and witnessed be seven persons or published as legislation in the Senate. When an important Roman died without living sons, it was common for him to adopt an heir in his will to take his estate, titles, and power, especially if the Roman citizen held an important position in society or the government. For example, Julius Caesar named Octavius as his adopted son and heir in his will. Octavius was able to use the appointment as Caesar's heir to support his claim to the Roman throne and eventually solidified his claim to be the first emperor of Rome by winning a bloody civil war against Marc Antony and Cleopatra.

Ancient Roman wills could be contested if the testator disinherited a child or left him or her nothing and didn't give a plausible reason for the action. However, if a Roman child was given any sort of legacy, no matter how small, that was considered proof the testator was of sound mind, had considered the child, and given him or her something, so the will was generally upheld. Some modern testators bequeath a dollar to a child they intend to disinherit, so it cannot be argued that he or she forgot a descendant. However, a will contest can still be brought for undue influence or incapacity by a modern disinherited descendant, even if he or she is given a token gift in the will. Roman law developed several formal requirements for a valid will.

Formal Requirements of a Roman Will

By the time of Emperor Justinian (fifth century AD), the formal requirements of a Roman will were standardized and required that the testator have the capacity to draft a will and that it had to be in writing, attested in the presence of seven witnesses, and published or passed as legislation by the Senate. Witnesses had to be free of any legal disability, so women and slaves could not attest a Roman will. A Roman citizen was forbidden by law from alienating all his property outside the immediate family. Natural heirs and descendants were entitled to inherit certain minimum assets under Roman law. A Roman male had to be over fourteen years of age to publish a will, whereas a Roman female could publish her will at twelve years of age. Prior to AD 439, all Roman wills had to be written in Latin. After that date, a Roman will could be written in Greek or Latin. When a Roman citizen died, his or her will was unsealed in the presence of an official called the praetor and validated through a formal procedure. Roman rules for validating a will were later borrowed by English and American probate courts.

In parallel with the development of Roman inheritance law, Jewish legal scholars developed their own rules of inheritance based on Roman law, the Old Testament, and Rabbinical teachings.

Ancient Jewish Inheritance Law

All Jewish people were encouraged to bequeath a portion of their estate to the temple in Jerusalem or a local synagogue when they died, and Jewish wills were often deposited in a synagogue for safe keeping until the testator died.[20] Inherited land was especially important among Jewish families, and their laws of succession were designed to help families retain title to ancestral land. For example, if a Jewish family was forced to sell inherited land because they were in financial distress, the family had the right to sell the land for a below-market price and redeem the land at a later date for the same low price. By law and custom, a Jewish man's primary heirs were sons born of his wife, and often a double portion went to the firstborn son according to biblical tradition. Illegitimate sons born to slaves, concubines, or prostitutes were not included in a Jewish man's inheritance at his death, and Jewish daughters were provided a dowry in lieu of a portion of their father's real estate.

If a Jewish father had no sons, he would leave his estate to his eldest daughter, but she was required to marry within her father's clan to retain the land. If a Jewish man left no living sons or daughters, his heirs were his brothers, then his paternal uncles, and finally the nearest male kin within his clan.

Jewish Son's Inheritance

Upon the death of a Jewish father, the estate was generally divided among his sons. However, if some of his sons were underage, the other sons could decide to keep the estate intact until the youngest son came of age before dividing their father's assets. If a brother married but died childless, another brother was expected to marry the dead brother's widow, and their sons would inherit the dead brother's estate. Generally, a Jewish father's land was gifted to his sons, with the firstborn sometimes receiving a double share and the remainder of his sons receiving equal portions. However, a Jewish father could change the natural birth order of his sons by declaring that a younger son was his "firstborn," and the newly declared firstborn son would then receive a double share of the estate following biblical traditions.

If a Jewish father was married to several women, he could not change the birth order of his sons—presumably because that would cause too much resentment and fighting among his wives. Early Jewish inheritance laws were later modified by Tannaitic rabbis to allow the gifting of land to wives and daughters during the father's lifetime as a way to avoid penniless widows and daughters.

Tannaitic Inheritance Laws

Tannaitic laws were developed and recorded in the first and second centuries AD.[21] The major difference between Tannaitic inheritance laws and earlier Jewish laws of succession was that the father's estate was required to be partitioned rather than inherited as a single entity owned jointly by all his sons, as was the case under some interpretations of early Jewish laws of succession. The belief that a Jewish father's estate should be partitioned rather than inherited as a single entity was probably derived from Roman inheritance laws, where a father's land was divided among all his sons and sometimes among his daughters.

Tannaitic law recognized two ways for a father to transfer property to his children: by gift during his lifetime or by inheritance under intestate laws after his death.

Gifting

Gifting during a Jewish father's life was voluntary and unconstrained by law, whereas inheritance was determined by Jewish intestate laws of succession. A gift during a father's lifetime could be refused, but an inheritance had to be accepted. Moreover, gifts could be given to nonfamily members, but an inheritance could not pass outside the decedent's family. Gifting of assets during a father's lifetime was intended to make contesting the gift after the father's death difficult. Gifting transferred only the father's property to the beneficiary, whereas inheritance transferred the father's property and all his other rights and powers associated with ownership of the land, including control over the family as head of household and any debts associated with the real property.

Tannaitic law recognized three different types of gifting: a gifting conditional on death, a completed gift of ownership of the land while the father was living with a retained use of the land during his lifetime, and a gifting that became effective when the father was on his deathbed. Gifting allowed a father to circumvent the rules of intestate succession and avoid giving all his land to his sons or a double portion to his eldest son. Gifting was likely borrowed from early Roman legal practices.

Gifting and Intestate Succession

The major differences between gifting and intestate inheritance are that gifting was a bilateral transaction between father and beneficiary that required the recipient to accept the property, whereas inheritance was a unilateral automatic transfer of title to land by law from the father to an heir at the father's death and could not be refused. Gifting required an intentional act whereas inheritance was governed by law and happened automatically on the father's death. Inheritance transferred title and use of the land and all obligations and rights owned by the father at the time of his death, including any debts owed or loans due to the father and leadership of the family if that right was associated with the inherited real estate. Gifting was generally not challenged in court, but the distribution of an estate at the father's death could be disputed if the beneficiaries weren't satisfied with what they received. Gifts of land brought any debt associated with it, and the recipient had to accept the land subject to the debt or refuse the gift. Gifting was done by preparing a written deed to transfer the land while the father lived.

Early Jewish inheritance laws resulted in heirs jointly owning the inherited land in common, and the eldest son inherited leadership of the family. This procedure made sense when the family kept the ancestral land together and several generations of the family lived in one large building on the land (similar to Chinese living arrangements). The firstborn Jewish son generally administrated the land owned jointly be the family and became head of the household when his father died. Jewish laws of gifting and intestate succession closely parallel ancient Roman laws of inheritance. In Roman and Jewish laws, gifting was bilateral and required the recipient to affirmatively accept the gift.

In early France and England, the church managed marriage, divorce, drafting of wills, probate, and estate administration.

French Inheritance Law

Before the French Revolution, different inheritance laws applied to aristocrats, middle-class Frenchmen, foreigners, members of the clergy, and commoners. Males were favored over females, older sons were favored over younger siblings, and illegitimate children could not inherit from their father. In addition, there were different rules of inheritance for various types of land, such as land held in fee simple versus land held in feudal tenure. Finally, inheritance laws varied in different regions of France prior to the revolution.

The French Revolution brought significant changes to society and the law, unified inheritance laws for aristocrats and commoners, treated all children equally, abolished feudal tenure, and applied the same laws of succession to all parts of the country. The goals of these new laws were to treat every Frenchman equally and to divide large estates among many descendants to dilute the power of rich aristocratic families. The new laws forbade a French father from disinheriting his children. If a father had no surviving children, the estate was divided among his siblings, nephews, and nieces. If he left no surviving siblings, nephews, or nieces, the estate went to his parents and then cousins. There was no provision for a surviving spouse in the new revolutionary inheritance laws because widows were taken care of by a contract negotiated and signed prior to marriage.

Napoleon changed French laws of inheritance when he took power.

The Napoleonic Code

When Napoleon seized power in 1804, he reformed French inheritance law, changing both intestate succession and the law of wills.[22] Under the Napoleonic Code, beneficiaries inherited both a testator's estate and his titles and powers without need of an administrator. The code regulated who would receive a testator's estate and forbid the disinheriting of children. The Napoleonic Code also allowed a testator to bequeath half his estate by will if one child survived, a third of his estate by will if there were two surviving children, and a fourth of his estate by will if three or more children survived his death. The Napoleonic Code was little changed for generations. Recent changes in the code involved the rights of surviving spouses and illegitimate children.

The Napoleonic Code was designed to keep ancestral lands within the father's family, so French inheritance laws discouraged passing land to a surviving widow. This neglect of surviving widows in French inheritance law was changed in 1891, when a statute was passed giving a surviving widow one-quarter of her dead husband's land for use during her lifetime, though no ownership of his real property. An illegitimate child could not inherit from his or her father under the Napoleonic Code unless legally recognized, and even then, if the parents had legitimate children, the recognized illegitimate children could take only one-third the share he or she would have received as a natural born child of the marriage. It was not until 1972 that French inheritance law allowed illegitimate children to share equally in their parent's estate with legitimate children. French law authorized the drafting of wills to distribute part, but not all, of a decedent's estate.

French Wills

There are three authorized types of wills in France: a holographic will drafted entirely in the handwriting of the testator, a formal will executed before a notary, and a mystic will that was signed by a testator, sealed, and delivered to a notary.[23] The notary described the mystic will process in writing on the face of the sealed will, and then the sealed will was signed by the testator, notary, and witnesses, to be opened after the death of the testator. Beneficiaries and relatives cannot be witnesses to a French will. Ordinarily, oral wills are not recognized in France, but oral soldier's and sailor's wills are allowed by special rules.

The history of English inheritance laws is described in the next chapter.

CHAPTER 2

English Inheritance Law

Anglo-Saxon rules of succession prior to the Norman Conquest were based on early German traditions, Catholic canon law, and Roman inheritance practices (Rome controlled Southern England until AD 410).[24] Written records of inheritance customs from Anglo-Saxon England have survived, so historians have a reasonable idea of what happened to property when an owner died during that period. The evidence comes mainly from statements about land succession recorded in the Domesday Book (a survey of land holdings ordered by King William in 1085, and the most extensive record of a preindustrial society in existence), copies of laws passed by Anglo-Saxon kings, and private annotations of inheritance rules maintained by wealthy Anglo-Saxon households. How Anglo-Saxons selected their kings illuminates the way inheritance customs worked in Anglo-Saxon England.

Succession to the English Throne

Evidence of Anglo-Saxon inheritance customs can be found in Beowulf, where succession to the English throne is described. Succession to power could happen in two ways: one derived from early German tradition about who should become king when a ruler died, and the newer Christian idea of hereditary royal succession.

Early German settlers in Anglo-Saxon England worshiped pagan gods, whereas later settlers in Roman England followed Christian teachings. The German tradition held that a king could choose his successor from among several candidates, both within and outside his immediate family. Moreover, according to German tradition, anyone could seize power by force if he was strong enough because competence and aggressiveness were admired. Within the Christian tradition, the throne passed to a dead ruler's firstborn son, or his next younger brother if there was no surviving son, because Christians believed God selected their kings.

Divine Right to Rule

After the eighth century, most English kings adhered to the Christian tradition that the firstborn son of a sitting king had a divine right to rule, believing that God made kings by birth. The danger in the German tradition of succession was that any powerful lord could make a claim to the throne if he possessed sufficient forces to seize control of the kingdom—often leading to bloody and destructive civil wars. Christian doctrines of hereditary monarchy were intended to avoid these problems and leave the selection of kings to God. Of course, the Christian doctrine of hereditary succession sometimes resulted in a king who was weak or intellectually limited, and at times sons and uncles competed for the English throne in spite of Christian doctrines.

In addition to Anglo-Saxon customs of inheritance and Christian theories of the divine right of kings, royal privileges developed in various parts of England after unification by King Alfred.

Custom and Royal Privilege

After unification of England, conflicts developed between ancient Anglo-Saxon inheritance practices and royal privileges granted by English kings to favored lords. The enforcement of local customs was the responsibility of assemblies elected by the local community while the enforcement of royal privileges rested with the king. Ancient Anglo-Saxon customs controlled the ownership of land, the inheritance of real property, and the enforcement of contacts. However, these local customs could be overruled by grants of privilege from English kings, especially after Alfred of Wessex united England in the ninth century. Favored lords were granted special rights to pass their property to kin and often received the right to levy fines and collect taxes.

Anglo-Saxon nobles, clergy, and rich landowners received land from their king in return for important services and they could generally devise these lands by will. It's believed that Anglo-Saxons followed strict rules concerning the inheritance of land; it usually passed to sons. However, they could gift or will personal property to daughters, widows, and younger sons if they wished.

Eventually, royal privileges became widespread and more important than local customs in Anglo-Saxon inheritance law among the upper classes.

Anglo-Saxon Customs

Anglo-Saxon land was customarily divided among the owner's sons, with the firstborn having some preference, probably the right to select the best land and perhaps keep the family home. Parts of Anglo-Saxon England practiced gavelkin, where a lord's land was divided among his sons, but the firstborn son took his father's title and ruled the extended family. Another custom in other parts of Anglo-Saxon England was that the family home went to the youngest son, and the remaining land was divided among the other sons, with the oldest having first choice of the parcel he wanted. There were variations on these Anglo-Saxon inheritance customs in different parts of England.

Anglo-Saxon Intestate Succession

When a man died intestate (without a will), his lands were divided justly among his wife and children and near kinsmen according to ancient customs. Historical records suggest that in Essex, a father could divide his lands among his sons in unequal shares. Family land in Anglo-Saxon England was passed through the generations in a flexible way that gave primacy to sons, with some special privileges reserved for firstborn sons. In the absence of sons, a daughter might inherit the family land, although there are few examples of females owning inherited land in the historical records of Anglo-Saxon England.

Anglo-Saxon inheritance rules varied substantially by social class and gender.

Class in Anglo-Saxon England

Anglo-Saxons society was defined by social class.[25] At the top was a king who ruled the nation after King Alfred united England. Below the king were ealdorman, roughly similar to dukes, earls, and archbishops in later English history. These titles were not hereditary in Anglo-Saxon England but were conferred by the king on his friends or kin for important services. Below ealdorman were shire-reeves (root of our word *sheriff*), who collected taxes and kept order. Below the shire-reeves were thanes, equivalent to medieval knights, originally members of the king's bodyguard. Thanes were freemen who owned enough land to allow the owner to afford weapons for his men. Thanes led their followers in battle when called to arms by the king. The next lower level of Anglo-Saxon society were peasants, called ceorls. They were freeman who owned and worked a small farm or carried on a trade, such as carpentry, metal working, or weaving. The bottom of Anglo-Saxon society was occupied by slaves.

Women had few legal rights in Anglo-Saxon England.

Anglo-Saxon Women's Rights

Women were defined in Anglo-Saxon law according to their social class and marital status. Women of higher social class enjoyed more rights than peasants but were still ruled by men. As women moved from being single, through marriage, and into widowhood, they gained some independence and more legal rights. Unmarried girls were under the protection and control of their nearest male relative, usually their father or brother. Wives were under the control and protection of their husband while he lived. Only widows were able to exercise some independent control over their dependents and inherited land. Married Anglo-Saxon women owned property inherited or gifted from their family or husbands, but their rights in the land were limited. A widowed mother was due half the family's joint property, whereas a childless widow received a smaller share of the property owned by her deceased husband.

An Anglo-Saxon widow had the right to custody of her children, but a widow who remarried had to forfeit part of the inheritance from her first husband and might lose custody of her children. A widow could not remarry for a year after the death of her husband, presumably to protect the paternity of unborn children. Anglo-Saxon women could not be coerced into an unwanted marriage, and married women could appear in court and take an oath.

English kings granted royal privileges to followers and these often included the right to bequeath land by will.

Anglo-Saxon Wills

Anglo-Saxon wills were generally written in English, and many experts believe they were transcriptions of oral wills made by scribes because few Anglo-Saxons could read or write. Some wills named an administrator or guardian of a child to carry out the testator's wishes after he died. Most Anglo-Saxon wills were based on royal privilege, which enabled the grantor to dispose of his land and personal property in ways not usually permitted by Anglo-Saxon customs, and they were written in English or Latin.[26] The development and use of Anglo-Saxon wills were supported by the Catholic Church and followed practices developed by the Romans. Anglo-Saxons followed ancient

Roman customs concerning personal property, proscribing that the widow take a third, the children a third, and the church receive the remainder. This custom was generally followed in Anglo-Saxon England prior to the Norman Conquest. After 1066, King William introduced the doctrine of feudal tenure and substantially changed English laws of succession.

King William left early Anglo-Saxon inheritance customs intact for the Anglo-Saxons but imposed a system of feudal tenure on large parcels of land he confiscated from English "traitors" who fought against him in the Battle of Hastings. William gave these confiscated lands to Norman nobles as rewards for their services in conquering England and established a system of feudal tenure on the lands. Feudal tenure fundamentally changed English laws of inheritance governing land for upper class Normans.[27]

Norman Inheritance Laws

Historical records of inheritance during the Norman period show that succession was based on individuals rather than families, as was customary under Anglo-Saxon rule. Almost immediately after his victory over King Harold of England, King William announced to the conquered Anglo-Saxons that every child will be his father's heir, indicating that he did not plan to change inheritance customs for Anglo-Saxon Englishmen. However, King William made major changes to the laws of inheritance for Norman noblemen because he was concerned about revolts against his rule.

King William established a feudal system of land tenure in England following the conquest and used confiscated lands to reward his Norman knights and lords with large estates. The Norman feudal system made drastic changes in English inheritance laws, because holders of feudal land were no longer free to sell or transfer their land to anyone they chose when they died. Instead, they held the land as a feudal tenant rather than an owner and paid feudal fees to their king. Feudal land in Norman England had to be passed to the lord's eldest surviving son, who held the estate in feudal tenure for his own surviving firstborn son, and so on. Lords and knights were obligated to pass their feudal lands and all obligations associated with the land to their firstborn sons at death, including the duty to pay a feudal fee to the king and fight for him when called to arms. If a feudal lord left no surviving son, his land returned to the king and was given to another Norman noble.

Feudal Tenure

Norman inheritance laws placed severe restrictions on who could inherit feudal land. The usual restriction was to own land by entail rather than fee simple, which involved owning an interest in land that was bound irrevocably to the grantee (recipient of the deeded land) and his direct descendants. Feudal land could not be sold or gifted to anyone outside the bloodline of the owner and had to pass intact to his oldest surviving son. Entailed land passed automatically to the firstborn son at his father's death. If a feudal tenant died without a direct male descendant, the land reverted to the grantor (the earlier holder of the land, usually the king) and was passed to another Norman lord in feudal tenure. Holding land in entail prevented the breakup of large English estates.[28] It also produced the English doctrine of primogeniture—the inheritance of the entire estate by the firstborn son. Primogeniture was not abolished in England until 1925. Most American colonies abolished primogeniture when they formed the Continental Congress.

Primogeniture

Primogeniture is the right of succession belonging to a father's firstborn son. Birth order and gender were crucial in the inheritance laws of Norman England because land passed to the eldest son of a dead landholder by operation of law.[29] Younger sons of lords and knights were generally given a small inheritance of personal property and left to fend for themselves by entering the clergy or serving in the military. Daughters were usually married to wealthy sons of aristocratic families and given a dowry from their father's personal property. A few lords and knights tried to soften the financial blow of primogeniture by gifting small plots of land to younger sons and money to their daughters during their lifetimes, but the eldest son still inherited the father's real estate, his title, any offices he held, and the duty to raise soldiers and lead them into battle if called to arms by the king. Passing real property and titles to the firstborn son kept large English estates intact so the Norman lord or knight would have sufficient wealth to maintain a large army ready to fight for his king at a moment's notice in case of rebellion or invasion.

Primogeniture often impoverished younger sons and daughters, who inherited little or nothing from their wealthy father. Norman daughters were forced to accept arranged marriages to enhance the political and social connections of their father, and younger sons entered the clergy or military to support themselves. Primogeniture created a difficult succession puzzle, however, when the firstborn son died before his father and left a son of his own.

What if the Firstborn Son Died?

Succession could become complicated if a firstborn son died, leaving a younger brother and a minor son of the deceased firstborn son as potential heirs to the land and title. Who would inherit—the adult younger brother or the minor son of the father's firstborn son? Anglo-Saxon laws would have given the land and title to the surviving younger brother of the firstborn son because he was an adult and could immediately rule the land and offer armed service to his king. However, after the Norman Conquest, the minor son of the dead eldest son inherited the land and title rather than the younger adult brother of the dead firstborn son. Catholic Normans believed that only God made heirs, and rulers should not be made by laws or court rulings. As a result, they followed the natural lineage from the father's oldest son to the oldest son's oldest son and so on until they found an heir. Only if the eldest son had no sons of his own would the younger brother of the deceased firstborn son take the father's title and land in feudal tenure.

Norman wills were of little importance in ancient times because they controlled only the distribution of personal property, which was minor compared to the importance of titles and land. It didn't take long for clever lawyers to figure out ways to defeat these strict Norman inheritance laws governing land, however. English lawyers developed a procedure called common recovery to transform land from feudal tenure to fee simple ownership through legal action in the common-law courts.

Common Recovery

Legal restrictions on the inheritance of land could be contested by a process called "the practice of common recovery," which involved a third party bringing suit against the entail tenant, claiming the third party had a good and valid right to the land.[30] The third party, called a common voucher, said he was ready to defend his claim to title in court and would set the case for trial. By prior agreement, the existing entail tenant would not appear in court, so the judge was forced to announce that the entail owner had defaulted on his claim and the land had to be transferred in fee simple to the third-party friend who had contested title to the land. By prior secret agreement, the entail tenant would recover his land from the third-party common voucher and now own the land in fee simple. This legal process allowed feudal restrictions on land ownership to be converted by operation of law into a fee simple ownership so the owner could now dispose of the land by will, gift, or sale to a third person outside his family. Common recovery was used widely by the fifteenth century to avoid restrictions on the inheritance of feudal land—and it worked fine so long as the third-party friend was trustworthy and returned the land to its rightful owner.

To limit the use of common recovery, a new legal device was developed, called the strict family settlement agreement, negotiated and signed when the eldest son married.

Strict Settlement Agreements

The main purpose of the strict settlement agreement was to keep feudal property intact and in the same family for generations.[31] A strict settlement agreement restricted the eldest son's ability to convert feudal tenure into fee simple ownership of land through the legal tactic of common recovery. Strict settlement agreements made generous financial provisions for younger sons and daughters and relieved the mounting pressure to abolish primogeniture in England. The strict settlement agreement included marriage portions for daughters and lump-sum grants or life annuities for younger sons as incentives to sign the contract. The strict family settlement was used extensively, beginning in the seventeenth century, to maintain large land holdings within English families and avoid the conversion of feudal land to fees simple ownership by the process of common recovery, allowing the sale of land to outsiders or its division among several sons when a father died.

The strict settlement agreement conferred specific rights on the wife, daughters, and younger sons born of the marriage and listed the property they would receive from their father's estate at maturity. The firstborn son effectively became a life tenant of the family's property. Strict settlement agreements guaranteed that the father's land and the aristocratic title associated with the estate would remain intact within the same family for generations and pass to the eldest surviving son. These strict settlement agreements also included clauses assuring the bride's family that any offspring of the marriage would be supported by the husband's family and would not become a burden on the bride's family in later generations, although the bequests to younger sons and daughters were still small compared with the huge grant to a firstborn son.

Primogeniture was not abolished in England until the twentieth century, when Parliament passed the Settled Land Act.

The Settled Land Act

Primogeniture remained part of English inheritance laws from the Norman Conquest in 1066 until 1925 when the Settled Land Act was passed by Parliament.[32] Over the centuries, some English land was transformed to fee simple ownership (meaning the owner could sell or will the land to anyone) rather than subject to feudal tenure restrictions (where the land could only be passed to the surviving firstborn son) by using the legal device of common recovery. But large tracts of English land were passed by primogeniture for centuries.

As more English land came to be owned in fee simple, the will became an important way to pass real property from one generation to the next.

Origins of Probate and Wills

After the Norman Conquest, written wills lost much of their importance among the Norman upper classes because land was subject to feudal tenure and passed automatically to the eldest surviving son. Only personal property could be gifted by will at death among Normans nobles. Pressure from the church and civil courts to formalize the laws of personal property inheritance and the drafting of wills led to the requirements that an executor be named in a will and that wills be probated. Later, when land could be passed by will, a method of authenticating wills was needed. To meet this need, the English legal system borrowed the procedure of probating wills from the Roman practice of having witnesses affix their seals and inspect them when the will was opened following the Roman testator's death.

The naming of an executor to handle the administration of an estate after the testator's death was borrowed from Byzantine and Mohammedan law. After the Catholic Church gained political power in England, ecclesiastical courts required that a third-party executor be appointed when the will was drafted to serve as a fiduciary agent for the decedent by probating and administering his will. Church courts would not validate a will unless an executor had been named, so the decedent effectively died intestate if his will didn't name an executor.

Inheritance of Land and Chattels

Following the Norman Conquest, the laws of succession for land and personal property diverged. Church courts had jurisdiction over the validity of wills, common-law and chancery courts oversaw the inheritance of land, and church courts exercised primary jurisdiction over the inheritance of personal property. During the Anglo-Saxon period, the inheritance of personal property was governed by customs and didn't require a will—a widow received one-third or one-half her husband's personal property if he died leaving sons, who each received a roughly equal share of the remainder. After the Norman Conquest, rules governing the inheritance of land were changed, but the laws concerning the inheritance of personal property continued to follow Anglo-Saxon customs. Thus, Englishmen were able to gift or will their personal property to anyone when they died, usually to younger sons and daughters, whereas feudal land passed to the eldest surviving son.

Church courts modified the rules for personal property inheritance to attract more bequeaths to the Catholic Church. The church focused first on the distribution of personal property owned by rich clergy, who were expected to distribute their personal property to charities and their church by a written will. Church members were also encouraged to draft a will leaving part of their personal property to the church. Dying intestate was considered a sin because it was believed the decedent had not accepted the ministrations of the church at death by willing property to the church. When a church member left no valid will, the crown, feudal lords, municipalities, bishops, and the pope competed for the decedent's personal property.

Wealthy merchants who died leaving mostly personal property and no will had part of their property claimed by the king and the church. No matter who ultimately took an intestate's personal property, the church administered its distribution and worked to change the laws of inheritance so a significant share of the decedent's personal property would pass to it.

As English wills became more important, the rules of drafting a valid will became more formal.

Formal Will Requirements

In mediaeval times, an Englishman's last will had to be voluntarily drafted by a competent testator, disclose the property owned, be notarized, be attested by the testator's seal, and bear the attesting seals of witnesses and an executor.[33] Although no formal language was required to make it valid, English wills generally began by bequeathing the decedent's soul to God and his body to a specific church for burial, included detailed funeral arrangements, contained a direction to pay the decedent's lawful debts, and included a list of chattels (personal property) to be given to friends and family.

Many features of early English wills were borrowed from ancient Roman law, but differences evolved as English courts became more experienced and sophisticated.

Roman and English Wills

Chief among the differences between Roman and English wills was that a Roman will had to be complete or it failed, whereas an English testator who died with an incomplete will could have the will carried out and the balance of his estate distributed according to the laws of intestate succession. Under Roman law, a testator had to name an heir or the will was not valid, but that was not true in English inheritance law. A Roman testator had to be a citizen rather than a slave or heretic, whereas under English law, the only requirement was that the testator be an adult and competent to draft a will. All of a modern testator's property (both personal and real) can be distributed through a will, but that was not true under Roman law, except for soldiers' wills. Early Roman wills were informal and didn't have to meet strict statutory requirements to be valid, whereas an English will had to meet statutory guidelines to be accepted for probate. Finally, a Roman will controlled a testator's estate from the time it was published, but an English will became effective at a testator's death. Jurisdiction over English wills was shared by different court systems over the centuries.

Jurisdiction over Wills

Two parallel court systems developed in England after the Norman Conquest: church courts that controlled the probate of wills and the distribution of personal property, and secular civil courts that handled land disputes.

The jurisdiction of church courts over matters of succession was extensive in England, including claims to personal property by the church itself.[34] Bringing a matter before an ecclesiastical court required the will be validated by evidence that it was the decedent's last will and was property executed (similar to modern probate procedures). Historically, lords of the manor had exercised probate jurisdiction, but ecclesiastical courts took over this function as the Catholic Church became more powerful after the Norman Conquest. Once church courts determined that a will was valid, beneficiaries looked to the crown to enforce their rights when title to land was disputed. Generally, a sheriff would carry out the distribution of personal property under a will, but if the will was contested, the dispute about personal property went before an ecclesiastical court for resolution by a church judge.

Church Courts

Most of the testamentary rights that existed in medieval England were the result of ecclesiastical courts' attempts to shift control over the inheritance of personal property to people who could be induced to donate part of the personal property to their church. A feudal tenant received his land from the king and could not devise his real estate to anyone because the land passed automatically to his eldest surviving son when the lord died. English children inherited from their father because all property owned by their mother was automatically transferred to the father when she married.

Jurisdiction over wills disposing of personal property resided in the ecclesiastical courts.

Ecclesiastical courts recognized an executor as the representative of heirs for probate and administration of an estate and supervised estate administrators to make certain the intent of the testator was fulfilled and the executor didn't defraud the beneficiaries named in the will. By the fifteenth century, courts of chancery were competing with ecclesiastical courts for probate jurisdiction and eventually chancery courts claimed limited jurisdiction over probate matters. This happened because creditors could not question accounts submitted to ecclesiastical courts, so they searched for and found a remedy in courts of chancery by bringing their claims before the crown. Modern probate courts gradually exercised jurisdiction over all wills, including their validity and construction.

The inheritance of land and personal property developed along different lines in Norman England. A lord's land generally went to his eldest son\, one part of his personal property went to his widow, one part went to the children, and one part went to the church or king. Moreover, when a testator made a will that contained no provisions for his widow and children, the document was generally overturned by the courts, and the family was protected by receiving their customary share of the father's personal property.

Disposition of Land

After the Norman Conquest, feudal land could not be bequeathed by will—feudal real estate passed automatically by law to the tenant's oldest surviving son. It was not until 1540 that the English Parliament passed the Statute of Wills, making land held in fee simple (rather than feudal tenure) legally disposable by will. The church could not own land, and married women, infants, idiots, and lunatics could neither own land nor write a will. After 1677, when the Statute of Frauds was passed by Parliament, wills had to be in writing and signed and dated by the testator before three or four witnesses. An existing will became void if a testator married or had a child after the will was written and executed because his circumstances had changed significantly, and he was required to draft and execute a new will to control the distribution of his estate.

Disposition of Personal Property

An Englishman could dispose of all his personal property by will if he left no wife or children, but only half his chattels if he was married or had children. Wills disposing of personal property could be made by males of fourteen and females of twelve years of age after consent. A will disposing of personal property need not follow strict statutory guidelines, and even oral wills were valid for disposing of personal property prior to 1838, except when the gift was valued at more than thirty pounds. A will in the testator's own handwriting was valid even if not signed because its authenticity could be ascertained from the testator's handwriting alone.

Historically, Anglo-Saxon sons shared their father's land equally, widows were given dowers, widowers received curtesy (a right to hold certain land inherited by his widow), and daughters received a dowry prior to marriage or after their father's death. These customs made the English family secure in its rights to land and personal property before the Norman Conquest. After the conquest and the introduction of feudal tenure and primogeniture, Norman nobles did not participate in these equitable inheritance rights. Instead, Norman nobles held their land in feudal tenure, and it passed automatically to the eldest surviving son at the father's death—leaving the widow, daughters, and younger sons only portions of the father's personal property. Freedom of alienation of land gradually developed alongside the feudal system of land tenure in England and gave testators some ability to take care of their families, but the Norman laws of succession did not produce equity in the distribution of an estate due to the doctrine of primogeniture, which lasted in England until 1925.

Englishmen gradually became dissatisfied with feudal laws of inheritance and wanted the ability to pass their land by will. In response, Parliament passed the Statute of Wills.

The Statute of Wills

After 1500, the English parliament began passing statutes modernizing the inheritance of land and personal property as more land was freed from feudal control and merchants began to accumulate significant personal property. As a result, wills became a significant way to distribute land and personal property. The Statute of Wills allowed decedents to pass land owned in fee simple (land not subject to feudal tenure) to beneficiaries by written will.[35] In 1670, another statute was passed by Parliament to control the inheritance of personal property when there was no written will (intestate succession). Under this new law, widows received one-third of all personal property owned by the husband/father, and children inherited the remaining personal property in equal shares. If no children survived from the marriage, the widow took half, and the husband's closest relatives received the other half of his personal property.

The Statute of Wills reinforced a landowner's right to devise lands owned in fee simple by will (a practice was not available for land held under the feudal tenure system). However, the Statute of Wills didn't require the testator to write, sign, or even have his will read to him after it was drafted—which produced opportunities for fraud. Also, if a testator acquired land after he drafted his will, that land was not included in the existing document, so the old will had to be revoked and a new one drafted to cover the distribution of the newly acquired land—a complex procedure that was often overlooked by testators who didn't know the law.

To correct many perceived defects in the Statute of Wills, Parliament passed the Statute of Frauds in 1677. This new law contained formal requirements for the execution and witnessing of wills and any other document, such as a deed or contract that passed title to land.

The Statute of Frauds

Under the Statute of Frauds, the formalities for transferring land were listed in detail and required that any land contract be in writing to be enforceable. The statute applied to wills and required that they be signed by the testator and attested and subscribed by three or four credible witnesses.[36] It was not until 1837 that the distinction between land and chattels was eliminated in the common law of English inheritance; after that date, the same will could dispose of real and personal property and be enforced in one court.

CHAPTER 3

American Inheritance Law

During the American colonial period, family wealth consisted primarily of a family farm and livestock, so the laws of succession were concerned with passing these items from one generation to the next by will or intestate succession. The state and church were relatively weak during the colonial period, and there were few financial institutions, so colonists held little wealth in the form of stocks, bonds, or cash. Most colonial families owned a farm, a house, a barn, a gun, and animals, but little else. After the American Revolution, economic and social conditions changed, and insurance, energy, and transportation companies emerged, allowing Americans to accumulate wealth in the form of stocks and bonds in addition to land. However, for generations family farms were the major source of wealth for most Americans.

Colonial America

Because land was abundant in America, the English practice of primogeniture was replaced by a more equal system of land distribution to sons and daughters in most of the colonies, except for parts of the South where owners relied on slave labor to grow cotton and tobacco on large plantations. In England, daughters and younger sons generally inherited modest financial assets, and the family real estate and title went to the eldest surviving son. Personal property made up a small part of most estates during the American colonial period, so laws of succession were concerned primarily with the inheritance of family farms. Over time, land decreased in importance compared with stocks and bonds, especially in the Northern states. As financial institutions developed and manufacturing companies issued stocks and bonds, inheritance laws governing the distribution of personal property became more important.

Throughout the early years in colonial America and even after the Revolution, decedents rarely left wills. In the eighteenth century, almost all probated wills were drafted by white males, whereas by 1980, half of all probated wills were drafted by women. Over the centuries in America, the types of assets passed from one generation to the next changed from the family farm to houses, stocks, and bonds. Houses gradually became the most significant real estate owned by most Americans rather than the family farm of earlier centuries.

Colonial Inheritance

The ownership of land was concentrated among white males during the American colonial period, and owning land was the major way individuals accumulated wealth during that period. Because there were no large financial institutions in America to transform real property into cash, the only significant asset owned by most Americans before the Civil War was the family farm. The American economy was based on agriculture, barter, and the purchase, homesteading, and trading of land rather than manufacturing, paid work, and investing characteristic of modern America. There was abundant land available in America at low prices or for the taking if one was willing to improve it and build a cabin. As a result, the ownership of land was not concentrated among an aristocratic elite, except in a few Southern states before the Civil War where large plantations existed based on slave labor growing cotton and tobacco.

Land Was Plentiful

The easy availability of raw land caused American inheritance laws to evolve differently from English laws of succession—inheritance was more democratic in America. In spite of the different economic conditions in the two countries, American colonial inheritance law borrowed from English common law and included restrictions on who could draft a will. An American testator had to be eighteen years of age to draft a valid will, and if he or she didn't leave a valid will, the state would distribute the decedent's property according to intestate statutes. Some states awarded a surviving spouse one-half the family estate, no matter what the will said. For example, the State of Louisiana followed French law, which held that a testator could not alienate more than half his estate if children or parents survived him.

In colonial America, a husband's consent was required before a wife could draft a will.[37] Holographic wills were valid in most but not all American states, and most states required that a formal written will be signed, notarized, and witnessed by several attesting witnesses. Today, only two witnesses are now required to attest a will. Vermont was the last state to require three witnesses for a valid will, and that requirement was reduced to two witnesses in 2006. Wills are not generally registered with a probate court when they are executed, but the will must be probated following the testator's death in all American states. It's good practice to have a testator's signature notarized when drafting a will, although that's not required in all states.

Pennsylvania inheritance laws are a good example of early American laws of succession.

Pennsylvania Inheritance Laws

In the Pennsylvania colony, inheritance laws gave one-third of a man's estate to his wife and one-third to his children; the final third could be disposed by will.[38] Similar to inheritance laws in England at the time, Pennsylvania laws limited the rights of a testator to disinherit his wife and children. Later, the Pennsylvania Assembly passed a law giving the eldest son a double share of his father's estate, but that fell far short of the English practice of primogeniture, where all real property and titles owned by a decedent passed to his oldest surviving son. Over the years, colonial assemblies passed additional modifications to their inheritance laws, generally moving toward a more democratic form of inheritance rather than following the English rule of primogeniture. Up until the American Revolution, the colonies relied on English common-law precedent to interpret their statues when they were ambiguous; after gaining independence, America developed its own unique legal system.

Some American colonies passed laws giving children the right to inherit two-thirds of a decedent's estate if there was a surviving spouse, and all of the estate if there was no surviving spouse when a father passed without leaving a will. Economic conditions in the American colonies, where cheap land was available to anyone who was willing to establish a homestead, made the idea of primogeniture largely irrelevant. In addition to ignoring the English rule of primogeniture, the American colonies never developed the practice of drafting strict family settlement agreements common among English aristocratic families, which were negotiated and signed at the time the eldest son married. A strict family settlement prescribed that the eldest surviving son held only a life estate in the land and title he inherited from his father, and he was required to pass the same land and title to his male lineal descendants in strict birth order upon his death.

The rights of women to own, manage, and inherit land were slow to develop in the Western world, although women's rights progressed faster in America than in most European countries.

Colonial Women's Rights

At marriage, ownership of woman's property automatically transferred to her husband in colonial America. A husband could manage her property but not sell it.[39] A woman's inherited land passed to her children when she died. American colonial women could draft wills distributing their personal property, but only if their husbands consented and approved the will. Most American colonial laws said little about the order of succession if a decedent left no lineal descendants. In those colonies that had statutes covering this contingency, the eldest brother usually took the decedent's real estate, especially among Southern colonies that wanted to keep land within the family to perpetuate large tobacco and cotton plantations.

American colonial inheritance laws generally required that men make provisions for their wives in case of death because husbands gained control of all their wives' property when they married. When American colonial males drafted a will, over half of them distributed more to their spouses than the share required by intestate statutes. When a husband limited his wife's inheritance, he generally gave her a life estate in real property to compensate for the smaller award of personal property. Under these conditions, a widow could not sell the land but could enjoy its use while she lived and then leave the land to their children when she died. Men wanted to keep land in the family and pass it on to their children when both spouses died. Rich men tended to leave a larger share of personal property to their wives compared with poor testators.

In a few states, women acquired the right to own and inherit assets during the early years of the United States, especially where inheritance laws interacted with a state's community property laws to influence how assets were passed from one generation to the next. States that followed the Spanish community property tradition gave women significant inheritance rights because women owned half the assets acquired during a marriage according to community property rules. Women in these states gradually gained more control over their financial affairs and earned the right to own land, draft wills, and manage their own finances independently of their husbands.

English and American Colonial Laws

Two major differences developed between English and American inheritance laws after the revolution. The first was that most

American colonies divided the estate among all lineal descendants rather than following the English doctrine of primogeniture, which awarded all real property and any titles to the eldest surviving son. The other difference was that American colonial families made little or no use of the strict family settlement agreement to bind the family land inherited by a newly married eldest son to the lineal descendants of the father. In some American colonies, if a white male didn't like the way his colony's intestate laws distributed property, he could draft a will giving his estate to whomever he wanted, including disinheriting his sons and daughters. Only the wife's claim of dower (a lifetime income from the real property of her deceased husband and the right to occupy the family home during her lifetime) could not be disturbed by will in the American colonies.

Approximately half of wealthy white males who owned large tracts of land drafted wills in colonial times. Generally, these wealthy landowners gave a larger share of their real estate to sons, but some colonial fathers distributed real property to their daughters as well. Often these bequests were financially smaller than intestate statutes prescribed, but they still involved the gifting of more land than younger sons and daughters would have received under the English doctrine of primogeniture.

Sons of colonial landowners generally benefited when a colonial father drafted a will that distributed less than the intestate laws prescribed for his widow. When colonial males distributed roughly equal shares of their estate to sons and daughters, they generally left land to their sons and personal property to their surviving spouse and daughters.

Post-Revolutionary Inheritance Laws

After the American Revolution, the US judicial system shifted away from relying on English common law and began developing its own precedents. America never established chancery or church courts because they were seen as tools of oppressive kings and a powerful state church. A few states, mainly in the South, did allow the use of entail deeds to limit the inheritance of land to lineal descendants prior to the American Civil War, allowing aristocratic Southern families to keep large plantations worked by slaves intact within the family.[40]

The American states developed civil courts at the county level to administer justice in disputes over the inheritance of land or personal property. Federal courts in America have no jurisdiction over inheritance laws.

American Inheritance Laws

After the American Revolution, some states passed laws requiring roughly equal division of a testator's estate among his children to encourage democracy and differentiate America from England's class-based society. The newly established American states wanted to promote wide ownership of land and felt one way to do that was to give each son an equal share of his father's land. However, some Southern states continued to favor the eldest son by giving him a double share of the family estate, and a few Southern landowners gave all their land to the firstborn son to keep the plantation intact within the family. When a plantation was distributed equally among sons of a Southern landowner, one son would often buy out the others so the family plantation would remain large enough for raising tobacco or cotton using slave labor. This process was made easier by the development of banking, so loans were available to the eldest son with land, slaves, and crops as collateral.

After the Civil War, primogeniture disappeared in America because the slaves were freed and large plantations were no longer economically viable. Most state laws also defined dower (the legal share of a husband's estate that a widow received on his death) and escheat (the conditions under which an estate would pass to the state). A decedent's estate passes to the state only if there are no known descendants or relatives of the deceased person living at the time of his death. Most states also allowed a widow to renounce her husband's will and take a specified amount of his estate under intestate succession laws in lieu of what the husband bequeathed in his will. Statutory inheritance laws also made it more difficult for a father to disinherit a son or daughter after the revolution.

There were few laws protecting the inheritance rights of illegitimate children among the American colonies, however.

Illegitimate Children

Children born out of wedlock in colonial America couldn't inherit from their biological parents unless one of them drafted a will gifting a portion of the family estate to the illegitimate child.[41] Illegitimate adults could distribute their own estate to their descendants or to a spouse, but they could not inherit from their biological parents unless they had been legitimized. If an illegitimate adult died without leaving a spouse or children, his or her siblings or parents could not inherit the property—it went to the state.

Only colonial Virginia passed laws covering inheritance rights for illegitimate children. Virginia allowed an illegitimate child to inherit his or her intestate mother's estate or pass his or her estate to the mother at death if the illegitimate person left no surviving children. Illegitimate Virginia children were given inheritance rights superior to the mothers' own parents and siblings, but inferior to any legitimate children she produced.

In addition to passing laws requiring a more equal distribution of land among a man's descendants, the widow's share was also specified in most American state laws.

Widow's Rights

Once the states mandated dividing an estate equally among sons and daughters after their father died, a widow's dower became difficult to administer because it required the awarding of land to the surviving widow, and that meant surveying and dividing the real property—an expensive and time-consuming process. As an alternative, American widows were often gifted personal property in the form of stocks, bonds, and cash rather than land. Among some of the Southern states, laws allowed a widow to renounce her husband's will and take a specified share of his land and personal property if she chose, including some of the family slaves.

Because slaves were defined as personal property in the South, these states were forced to deal with the legal problems associated with distributing land and personal property to widows, sons, and daughters earlier than in Northern states, which only resolved these issues decades after the American Revolution. A white man's slaves were generally distributed equally to all his children in the Southern states because they were personal property. If a widow renounced her husband's will, she was guaranteed a share of his slaves according to intestate statutes. A few wealthy Southern plantation families used a variation of the English marriage settlement agreement to keep land within the family for generations. This was rare, however, because there was so much open land available in America that younger sons could simply buy or homestead new land further west, so there was less pressure to break up large Southern plantations.

Marriage Settlement Agreements

Prior to marriage, some wealthy American families negotiated and signed a marriage contract establishing separate property for a wife in case of divorce and support for her following the husband's death, often in the form of a trust. Sometimes these negotiated marriage settlements allowed the wife to manage and even gift her separate property and hold it exempt from claims by her husband's creditors. The practice of establishing separate property for the wife in a trust with a trustee to oversee the assets was designed to protect wives from coercion by their husbands, although marriage settlements could be established without a trust if the couple wished.

Allowing women to negotiate and sign a marriage contract helped them to attain some autonomy within marriage at an earlier time in American compared with Europe. Moreover, her separate property would be protected if a widow remarried after her husband's death, and her rights often included the ability to bequeath her separate property by will at her own death. Fathers also used trusts to protect a daughter's inheritance from her husband's control. Although a marriage settlement agreement conferred significant benefits on a wife, few couples actually drafted one because men traditionally made all family financial decisions.

After the Civil War, all American states abolished the doctrine of primogeniture because there were no slaves to work large cotton or tobacco plantations.

Abolition of Primogeniture

The most significant change from earlier inheritance practices in America after the Civil War was the abolition of primogeniture among a few Southern states, giving sons and daughters roughly equal rights to inherit from their parents. During the nineteenth century, evolving inheritance laws gave wives and daughters more rights to ownership and inheritance of property. After the Civil War, most states passed statutes giving women control over any property they inherited from their family of origin. Moreover, women gained the right to draft wills and gift their separate property to whomever they wished. Later, intestacy laws in most states gave daughters equal inheritance rights with sons, although that equality was slow in coming.

The states of Arizona, California, Texas, Idaho, Louisiana, Nevada, New Mexico, Washington, and Wisconsin brought the Spanish concept of community property with them when they joined the union, and this doctrine gave women significant rights to inherit community property during divorce or after the death of their husbands.[42]

Community Property Laws

In states that adopted community property laws, spouses jointly own the estate they accumulate during marriage. If they divorce or one spouse dies, different rules apply to the division and ownership of family assets, depending on whether the property was characterized as separate or community at the time it was acquired. Property acquired by gift, devise, or descent is always separate property, but all other property is presumed to be community property unless proved to be separate by clear and convincing evidence. A majority of American states followed the English common-law rule about ownership of property during marriage and at death, holding that the name(s) on the title of an asset determines how it should be distributed at divorce or death.

Because English common law recognized only the existence of a husband's separate property, during the early years of American independence, all assets acquired during the marriage were the separate property of the husband in those states that didn't follow Spanish community property rules. Only a husband could contract for and purchase real estate prior to the 1850s in America. At the death of the husband, the widow was entitled to an intestate share of his separate property or the share gifted to her in his will. As state inheritance statutes were gradually liberalized and women acquired the right to inherit and own separate property, husbands no longer gained control of their spouses' property at marriage and had to make do with only an intestate portion at the time of her death. Laws in states that followed the doctrine of community property benefited women greatly and contributed to American women attaining economic and legal rights earlier than in Europe.

After the Civil War, most American states passed laws giving equal intestate shares to the surviving spouse, whether male or female. In addition, most states gave surviving husbands and wives fee simple ownership of land (ownership forever) rather than just a life estate (use of the land for the life of the surviving individual) in inherited real property.

The State of Texas brought the concept of homestead to the United States when it joined the union, and the idea quickly spread to other states.

Homestead Laws

A significant addition to American inheritance law occurred with the passage of homestead laws exempting real property used as a primary residence by the family (a home or farm) and certain personal property necessary to work a farm, from attachment by creditors during bankruptcy or at the death of a husband.[43] This innovation was first passed by the State of Texas in 1839, soon after it joined the union, and was quickly copied by most American states. Also, many states passed laws allowing acknowledged illegitimate children to inherit from their father and mother, although only a few allowed a child to inherit from his or her father if the illegitimate child was not acknowledged. By 1890, most states allowed married women to own and bequeath property in their own name.

American laws of succession treated the inheritance of real estate and personal property in similar ways earlier than the English common law.

Reform Movement of 1850

As part of a reform movement in American law after 1850, several states abolished the doctrine of entail (the passing of land from one generation to another with the restriction that it must pass to a son in the family bloodline). However, by the time state legislatures got around to abolishing entail from land deeds, few testators were actually drafting wills requiring that land pass by entail rather than fee simple. The legislatures of several states also gave women the right to appoint a testamentary guardian for their children when she died. Some states revised their intestate statutes to give mothers the right to inherit from their children, and illegitimate or adopted children were included in the line of succession for the inheritance of property.[44]

Modern American inheritance laws were significantly affected by federal estate taxes and social security pensions.

Modern Inheritance Law

The introduction of a federal estate tax, the establishment of social security benefits for older individuals,[45] and other safety nets for seniors such as Medicare coverage when they reach age sixty-five[46] were major milestones in American inheritance law.

A major change in American inheritance laws occurred when Congress passed the estate tax in 1916.

Estate Tax

The reintroduction of a federal estate tax had a profound effect on how Americans structure their estates. The estate tax triggered an explosive growth in the drafting of family trusts and other estate planning strategies to minimize taxes paid to the federal government when a family member died. The US government had collected inheritance taxes during earlier financial and social crises, such as the panic of 1797 and during the American Civil War, to support financial institutions or pay for the enormous expense of maintaining the Union Army. But these earlier inheritance taxes were repealed after the crises passed. Not so with the modern federal estate tax, although recent increases in exemptions have limited the impact of America's estate tax on most families.

The highest estate tax rate was 10 percent when the original law was passed, and the first estate tax exempted property inherited by the spouse and children from taxation. However, during the Great Depression of the 1930s, higher progressive estate tax rates were introduced and have been with us ever since. In 1981, the Reagan administration and the US Congress lowered the highest marginal estate tax rate from 70 percent to 50 percent and increased the exemption from federal estate tax to $600,000. In 2020, the estate tax exemption was $11.58 million per person, meaning that only a few families faced the prospect of paying significant estate taxes. Another exemption allowed an inheritance to the surviving spouse to escape estate taxes during the spouse's life, effectively cutting the estate tax for married couples during the surviving spouse's lifetime. Also, because a surviving spouse was likely to spend a significant portion of the inherited estate on living expenses, the final estate tax paid was generally less than for single individuals who died leaving a similar size estate. In addition, generation skipping trusts allowed family wealth to escape estate taxation for generations, until this loophole was closed by Congress in 1976, requiring families to pay a gift tax on property given to grandchildren.

The original purposes of the federal income and estate taxes were to raise money to fund the government and reduce financial inequality among Americans. During the Great Depression rates of income and estate taxes became more progressive as a social engineering tactic to equalize wealth among Americans, raise money to support government programs designed to increase employment, and minimize financial resentment among the poor. Although the federal estate and income tax rates were made progressive and fairly high, the percentage of wealth actually paid to the federal government in estate taxes decreased after the Second World War because of exemptions introduced at that time, especially the larger exemption from estate taxes on inherited wealth, the marital deductions estate tax exemption, annual tax-free transfers of assets, and through generation skipping trusts drafted during the testator's life. Additionally, wealthy families established trusts and other complex estate plans to shelter some of their wealth from federal estate tax.

Another law that had a profound influence on inheritance in the United States is the Social Security Act of 1935, passed under the administration of Franklin D. Roosevelt.

Social Security

When Congress passed the Social Security Act, it was a financial tipping point for many older Americans. For the first time, the government accepted part of the financial burden of supporting elderly parents, relieving children and parents themselves from the stress of saving for retirement, planning and paying for life insurance, and continuing to work into old age. Prior to passage of the Social Security Act, many Americans continued to work well past age sixty-five. Even wealthy individuals didn't retire in those days; they merely decreased their work hours as they aged. Today, the majority of older Americans are retired and living on their savings and social security income by age sixty-five years—less than 20 percent of older Americans are working today. Before Social Security, estate planning was concerned primarily with taking care of a man's family when he died, through accumulated property and savings or a life insurance policy.

There are more Americans over sixty-five years of age today than in prior generations. The percentage of older Americans in the population has increased from under 4 percent to over 15 percent during the last generation. Because of Social Security pensions, elderly parents are less of a financial burden on their children. After the US introduced Social Security pensions, the amount of wealth parents pass to their children has grown because Americans have accumulated considerable wealth through investing. Also, they are spending less of their accumulated wealth to support themselves because older Americans can count on receiving a Social Security stipend every month, so more money is left to pass to their children. Because of Social Security pensions, significantly fewer older parents are moving back with their children, although today more children are moving back to their parents' homes rather than getting married and establishing their own families.

Modern estate planning is focused on caring for surviving family members who may be disabled or minors rather than estate tax avoidance, as was the case earlier.

Modern Estate Planning

Today, most older Americans are more concerned about planning for their own retirement than avoiding estate taxes when they die. The most notable changes in modern American inheritance law over the last generation have been an increase in the spousal share of inherited estates, more equal distribution of assets among sons and daughters of deceased persons, and the increased use of wills to transfer assets to the next generation. Most states no longer allow a testator to favor one sex over the other when he or she dies, and intestate statutes don't differentiate between male and female descendants, so sons and daughters generally receive equal shares of a family's assets at death when there is no will. Moreover, more decedents are leaving wills and living trusts to transfer their wealth to the next generation rather than relying on state intestate statutes to distribute their assets to their surviving spouse and children. In the past, trusts were used to minimize estate taxes.

Bypass Trusts

Before estate and gift tax exemption was raised, many couples drafted estate plans that included a bypass trust to take advantage of the 50 percent marital deduction introduced in 1948.[47] By placing 50 percent of the family estate in a bypass trust for support of the surviving spouse, he or she was able to postpone paying estate taxes on that portion of their assets until the surviving spouse died. Because the surviving spouse was likely to spend a significant portion of the estate on living expenses, the total estate tax bill when the surviving spouse died was substantially lower in many cases. Today, trusts are used primarily to support a surviving spouse or minor descendants when the other spouse dies.

Because common-law intestate statutes were not as generous to women as community property statutes, many testators give their widows a larger share of their estate at death through a will. Generally, testators who drafted a will left one-half of their estate to the surviving widow, rather than the one-third stipulated in many intestate laws. Over 90 percent of testators who have children pass their entire estate to their spouse and descendants and don't include collateral relations such as cousins or aunts and uncles in their wills.

Primogeniture was eliminated in American inheritance law after the Civil War, but some wealthy families still try to maintain their family fortune over generations by establishing family trusts that manage and distribute assets to children and grandchildren. The major changes in inheritance from colonial times to today has been a shift from the family farm to cash, stocks, bonds, and a home as the primary sources of wealth in modern American estates and the distribution of assets to the surviving spouse and all children rather than to the testator's sons.

CHAPTER 4

Probate and Will Contests

A modern will must be filed in a probate court to determine whether it is the valid last will and testament of the deceased person, has not been revoked or superseded, and was property executed. Once the will is validated, the probate court will issue letters testamentary appointing an executor to gather assets, pay legitimate debts, and distribute assets to beneficiaries according to the terms of the will.[48] The word *probate* derives from the Latin word *probatum*, which means established or proved. As applied to the laws of inheritance, probate has come to mean proof of the validity of a will filed with the court and the administrative process of collecting and distributing a decedent's assets to the proper beneficiaries. Statutory probate courts exist in larger American counties, whereas smaller counties assign probate jurisdiction to regular civil courts. The rights of heirs depend on establishing a will's validity, so it's important to file in the proper court.

In Anglo-Saxon England prior to the Norman Conquest, owners could bequeath their land by will.

Wills Gifting Land

Early Anglo-Saxon wills that devised land needed no validation by a probate court because the owner of real estate didn't need to prove the existence and validity of a will unless title to the land was disputed. An early Anglo-Saxon will that devised land was the equivalent of a modern warranty deed used to transfer title to land from a grantor to a grantee when sold or inherited. In early England, if title to land was contested, the will was produced in a common-law court and proved to be valid by attesting witnesses to prove ownership of land.

Most historians believe the modern procedure of probating a will derives from the ancient Roman practice of breaking the seals on a citizen's will before witnesses who originally attested to the document.

Origins of Probate

Early Roman wills had to be witnessed by six or seven persons, who affixed their seals to the will (called a will under seals). If an ancient Roman will was opened for any reason before the person died or after the death of the testator, a majority of the witnesses who had affixed their seals to the will had to be present at the opening, although a witness could send a friend instead if he could not attend the opening of the will in person for any reason.[49] The witnesses or their representatives had to establish that the seals were unbroken at the time the will was withdrawn to be opened. After an ancient Roman will was opened, the witnesses or representatives also had to state that they recognized their individual seals and were satisfied that the will was intact when it was opened and had not been changed—a procedure analogous to the modern probating of a will.

The court responsible for authenticating wills changed after King William conquered Anglo-Saxon England and introduced Norman law and feudal tenure to the country.[50]

The Norman Conquest of England by William changed the government, judiciary, and society of Anglo-Saxon England in many ways, including the English inheritance system and how land was held and passed from one generation to the next. Before the conquest, there were no ecclesiastical courts in England—the clergy filed their suits in secular law courts when they had a legal dispute. King William established ecclesiastical courts separate from common-law courts and assigned jurisdiction over the inheritance of personal property to ecclesiastical courts, but he left jurisdiction over the inheritance of land in common-law courts.[51] Laws governing the inheritance of land changed fundamentally after the introduction of feudal tenure by the Normans.

Norman Feudalism

After the Norman Conquest, King William established a system of feudal tenure over large tracts of confiscated land throughout England. Under the doctrine of feudalism, loyal Norman lords were given large estates to rule, but they didn't own the land; instead, they swore fealty to the king, paid him a feudal fee, and couldn't sell the property. A Norman lord held land during his lifetime, and it passed automatically to his oldest surviving son when the father died. Feudal lords and their tenants could be ordered to mobilize in case of war or rebellion and had a duty to defend the realm. The Norman king was the ultimate lord of all the land in this feudal system, but he distributed land to his loyal followers to support armed men in case there was an Anglo-Saxon rebellion. If a Norman lord died without heirs, the land returned to the king to be distributed to a new lord who would live on the land, cultivate it, and owe feudal fees and duties to the king.

Feudal land was passed by strict laws of succession to the eldest son.

Inheritance of Feudal Land

The feudal system forbade Norman Englishmen selling land or passing title as they wished at death. Instead, strict Norman laws of succession governed the inheritance of land: all real property owned by a Norman lord passed automatically to his eldest surviving son who succeeded to his father's land, titles, and feudal obligations to pay fees and supply military service to the king when his father died.

In contrast, personal property could be passed by will in England.

Inheritance of Personal Property

Norman inheritance law took little notice of personal property because it was much less important than ownership of land at the time, and King William was primarily concerned with having loyal lords own land sufficient to support a strong military defense in case of invasion or Anglo-Saxon rebellion. However, the Catholic Church was quite interested in how personal property was inherited because religious beliefs of that era dictated that a dying person should gift some of his personal property to the Church. It was a minor sin not to make a will and leave assets to the church, so ecclesiastical courts worked diligently to acquire jurisdiction over decedents' personal property and made certain the Church could administer the will and distribute the testator's personal property to his family and the church. If a decedent left a will, it was submitted to the Bishop's Court for validation and to oversee disposition of personal property according to the terms of the will. If there was no will, the local bishop would take charge of the dead man's personal property and distribute is in a suitable manner, making certain the Church received a portion of the dead man's personal property.

Church and civil courts shared jurisdiction over the administration of wills after the Norman Conquest.

Jurisdiction over Wills

Newly established ecclesiastical courts didn't have exclusive jurisdiction over wills after the Norman Conquest because creditors could sue the deceased person's estate in a common-law civil court and receive a judgment against his personal property for debts owed. Neither the ecclesiastical nor common-law courts were suited to handle these conflicting claims of creditors and heirs, so another judicial system evolved to handle judicial conflicts over a dead man's estate. This new court system was called the chancery court and grew out of the chancellor's administration of equity justice when a ruling from a common-law court was considered unfair by the king.

Chancery Courts

When there were conflicting claims to a dead man's personal property, jurisdiction over the dispute was often assigned to the chancery court for settlement if the king believed the common-law courts might produce an unfair outcome. Chancery courts heard evidence and ordered the administrator of the will to carry out its decision, or the chancery court took charge of the estate and disposed of it in a suitable way through its own administrative actions. However, the chancery court could not act until an ecclesiastical court had issued letters of administration to the executor of a will—a process handled by probate courts in modern England and America. Because bishops knew more about canon law than common law, the rules for probating a will were based primarily on ancient Roman law.

Ecclesiastical judges during the Middle Ages had to be a member of an order (a community professing a vow of poverty, chastity, and obedience, governed by a superior) and over twenty-five years of age, although they could be either brothers or priests. Ecclesiastical judges were trained in canon law and gained experience in ecclesiastical courts. In addition to a judge, each ecclesiastical court had a registrar to organize the docket and a scribe to keep records of court proceedings. The registrar determined the order and scheduling of trials before the ecclesiastical court. Modern probate procedures developed from these complex shared jurisdictions.[52]

Probate Procedures

In early English legal practice, proving the validity of a will and granting letters of administration were handled by church courts, and then the case was transferred to a civil court for administration or to a chancery court when there was a dispute the king believed was not suited to a common-law court. Proceedings in chancery courts were recorded in Ex Officio Act books by scribes and contained the name of the deceased, the names of executors or administrators, notice of a grant of execution on an inventory of the estate, the value of all goods in the estate, and any fees charged for services by the court or the administrator. These books also listed any claims against the estate, requests for the payment of the deceased person's debts, and other administrative documents connected with probating and administering a will.

The Catholic Church gradually lost power relative to secular kings, and the ecclesiastical courts' jurisdiction over wills and other matters associated with the inheritance of personal property diminished, although church courts retained power over the probate of wills into the nineteenth century in England. Litigants who were unhappy with the rulings they received from ecclesiastical courts could seek a writ of prohibition in a common-law court to stop a church court from carrying out its order. The proliferation of these writs of prohibition eventually burdened ecclesiastical courts so heavily they could not effectively function. To remedy this problem, chancery courts assumed jurisdiction over will administration, resolving the impasse and administering justice in a more efficient manner than the ecclesiastical courts had been able to accomplish because of conflicting jurisdictions.

Chancery courts flexible rules allowed judges to handle both personal property and real estate at the same time. However, chancery courts never assumed jurisdiction over the probate of wills or the appointment of administrators or executors; these actions remained within the jurisdiction of ecclesiastical courts. In modern times, jurisdiction over probate matters and the issuance of letters administration or testamentary is assigned to statutory probate courts or civil courts in England and America.

Probate courts in America developed differently from church and civil courts in England primarily because there was no state religion in the colonies.

Origin of American Probate Courts

Colonists in America followed English common law concerning laws of inheritance, including the Statute of Wills.[53] In contrast to the

English feudal system, however, primogeniture was never a significant part of the American colonial system of inheritance law, although practices similar to primogeniture developed in southern colonies because rich aristocratic families owned large plantations devoted to growing tobacco and cotton using slave labor. The American colonies conferred jurisdiction over wills to civil courts or the governor of the colony. Only in 1857 did the English Parliament transfer jurisdiction over probate and marital cases from ecclesiastical courts to the court of probate and the divorce court.[54]

Wills Gifting Personal Property

Ecclesiastical courts validated wills and administered the distribution of personal property to beneficiaries according to the terms of the will. These church courts were required to establish that the will had been properly executed by a competent testator following correct legal procedures before competent witnesses. Also, the church courts had to determine that the will had not been revoked and was in fact the last will drafted by the testator.

English legal practice developed two forms of probate: probate in common, where an executor produced the will and proved its validity by his own oath, and probate per testes, where all interested parties were given notice, attesting witnesses were called, and they were examined extensively by the ecclesiastical court. The formal probate method was more expensive and used only when the validity of the will was contested because of irregularities in its execution or unusual circumstances associated with the testator's drafting of the will (issues of testator competence or undue influence by third parties were common allegations).

Wills Gifting Land and Personal Property

An ecclesiastical court could examine the terms of a will concerning the testator's personal property, but the court had no jurisdiction over the disposition of land. If a beneficiary's title to land was questioned, his ownership of the land had to be proved in a court of common law.

The early history of American probate courts was different from English probate practice because in America, all probate matters were handled by civil courts. The colonies never established ecclesiastical courts because there was no state religion in America. Probate courts were established in populous counties, whereas in more rural counties civil courts handled probate maters along with other civil cases.[55] Additional statutory probate courts were added in counties where populations expanded in later generations. Long before the practice was adopted in England, American courts allowed the handling of wills dealing with land and personal property in a single probate or civil court.

Because wills can be revoked at any time prior to the testator's death, a will can't be probated until after the testator dies. Many beneficiaries would like to preserve evidence of the testator's competence and the absence of fraud or undue influence at the time the will is drafted by filing witness statements with a probate court, but there is no way to do that in America. Legal experts have proposed a law that would allow beneficiaries to call the testator as a witness in a probate court when he drafts his will to preserve the original document and provide evidence that it was property executed. However, probate courts have refused to take on that burden. Some states allow a will to be deposited in the probate court records to guard against alternation, loss, or forgery after the will is drafted and executed, and several states allow a self-proving affidavit be fixed to the will showing it was property executed. However, the deposited will must still be probated in a court of proper jurisdiction after the death of the testator.

Probate Procedures

An executor is generally required to produce the original will for probate.[56] If the executor neglects or refuses to offer a will for probate, another interested party, such as a beneficiary, can petition a court to accept the will for probate and name a new executor. Generally, the probate process is initiated by the executor's attorney filing a petition for probate of the will, but filing the will alone is sufficient to begin the probate process in a few states. Usually, the petition must allege that the testator is dead and was domiciled in the county where the case is filed prior to his or her death. Most probate courts require that interested parties be given notice of the proceeding before the probate court will schedule a hearing on the matter. If the will is not contested, the probate proceeding is fairly simple: a witness must testify that the testator has died and was domiciled in the county at the time of his or her death and that the will on file is the valid last will of the decedent. If a self-proving affidavit is attached, there is no need for additional witnesses to prove the will was property executed.

Self-Proving Affidavit

Many states allow self-proving affidavits be attached to the will so that witnesses need not be brought into probate court to testify personally about the execution of the will when the testator dies.[57] The self-proving affidavit is not available in the District of Columbia, Maryland, Ohio, and Vermont, so an attesting witness must appear and give evidence about the will's execution in those states and the District of Columbia. In California, Indiana, and New Hampshire, witness signatures on the will are adequate to prove it was properly executed without a self-proving affidavit.

What happens if an original will is lost?

Lost Wills

If an original will is lost, its terms can generally be established by submitting a copy of the will and testimony of persons familiar with the original will, such as the attorney who drafted it.[58] If a testator left a will, it must be probated because the beneficiaries cannot establish their claims to the testator's property otherwise. If there is no will, then the family must file an affidavit of heirship with the probate court to determine the rightful owners of the decedent's assets.

Any interested party may enter an appearance and contest the validity of a will by alleging a defect in its execution, lack of competence on the part of the testator, and undue influence or fraud in the drafting of the will. If a will is contested, the probate court must determine its validity before it can issue letters testamentary naming an executor. If a will is contested, a probate court will determine whether the testator had capacity to draft the will and whether there was undue influence or fraud involved before proceeding with administration.

Will Contests

Depending on the laws of the state involved, there are three ways to contest a will: directly in a probate court, by appeal of the probate court's order to a higher court, or by a separate action in a court of equity.[59] In fact, few wills are contested; legal experts estimate that under one percent of American wills are disputed. The statute of limitations for contesting a will begins to run when the will is filed for probate and is generally two years, but it can vary among the states. The grounds for contesting a will include allegations that it was not properly executed, the testator lacked capacity to draft a will, claims that the will was altered or forged, an allegation that undue influence was exerted on the testator at the time the will was drafted, a statement that the will was revoked, or the testator was operating under a mistake belief or delusion when he or she drafted the will that renders it invalid.

Contesting a will based on improper execution is rarely successful because if the will has a self-proving affidavit attached or is in writing, dated, signed by the testator, and witnessed by two or three competent persons, the execution procedure is almost always upheld by a probate court.

Any interested party who could expect to receive a benefit may file a will contest.[60]

Standing to Contest a Will

A will can be contested by heirs and beneficiaries. An heir who could expect to receive property under the state's laws of intestacy has standing to contest a will. Beneficiaries under a prior will can contest a later will, unless the contesting party's interest is the same or larger under the later will. A person who purchased property from an heir has standing to contest a will if the seller turns out not to be a named beneficiary of the offered will. However, creditors of the deceased person cannot contest a will in probate court. Instead, creditors must file their claims in the probate court with the executor and ask him or her to determine the validity of their claims on the estate before they can ask for a ruling from a probate judge on the validity of their claim if it's denied by the executor.

There are various forms of evidence that may be offered in a probate court to contest a will.

Evidence in a Will Contest

The person contesting a will must state his or her grounds for believing the will is improper and must show standing to bring the suit—in other words, the contestant must let the probate court know why they are contesting the will and show he or she is a person with an interest in the will who will be injured if the will is judged valid. There is no right to a jury trial in a will contest. A physician can be called to testify in a will contest when a testator's competence is questioned, because physician-patient privilege is waived so relevant evidence can be reviewed by the probate court. The attesting witnesses can be called to verify that proper procedures were followed in drafting and executing the will if execution is at issue—although that claim is rare. Experts can testify about the capacity of a testator to draft a will.[61]

Undue influence is usually proved by circumstantial evidence showing that the influencer had the opportunity to pressure the testator, the testator was susceptible to undue influence because he or she had a weak mind, the influencer was disposed to use his or her influence to alter the terms of the will, and the result of the contested will is different from what would normally be expected and appears to be the result of improper influence.[62]

Revocation of a will can be shown by mutilation of the will, a notation of revocation on the face of the document, evidence of a testator's intent to revoke the will, testimony that the original will cannot be found, or offering a later will for probate. Many attorneys try to protect against a will contest being filed by including a no-contest clause in the will, but most probate courts won't enforce a no-contest clause because they feel the contestant should have his or her day in court.

Bringing a will contest can cause division and bitterness within a family, and it's often not worth the trouble unless the estate is substantial. However, that doesn't dissuade disgruntled family members from bringing a will contest if they are unhappy with what they are likely to receive from the deceased person's will. Will contests are often filed over small amounts of property because the family members care so much about the issues involved and have residual emotional resentments leftover from earlier family interactions. Will contests generally are filed by disappointed or unhappy members of the decedent's family. Often, the filer is a child from a prior marriage, a second wife, or children who feel their father left too much money to his wife and not enough to them. Even if a contestant has standing, he or she needs a valid reason to bring a will contest. Claiming the will is unfair won't get one very far in a probate court. On the other hand, claiming that the testator lacked the capacity to draft a will, that the will is a forgery, that it was drafted under undue influence, or the testator acted under a mistaken belief about facts are valid objections to a will and reasonable bases for filing a will contest. Lack of capacity and undue influence are the most frequent claims filed in will contests.

Lack of Capacity

A testator lacks the capacity to draft a will if he or she is a minor, demented, or insane.[63] A person must be an adult to draft a will, and adulthood is determined by chronological age. An individual is considered demented if he or she cannot bring to mind the assets owned, cannot recall the natural persons who should benefit from the estate, and cannot correlate the assets and the persons who are the natural beneficiaries of the estate in his or her mind during the drafting of a will. Ancient Romans required that citizens be of age before they could draft a valid will, and that requirement has been adopted by all subsequent legal systems. Generally, the test has been applied to biological age rather than maturity or legal emancipation, so individuals need to be above a certain chronological age to draft a valid will. Dementia can render a will invalid even though the testator is of age if he or she is senile, lacks sufficient memory to be competent, or suffers some other emotional or intellectual deficit that precludes him or her making a valid will. Insane persons cannot execute a valid will because they don't have rational capacity, and older persons who suffer from dementia can't draft a valid will because they lack the ability to recall their assets and family.

Generally, expert testimony from the testator's physician or analysis of medical records is offered as evidence of dementia in a will contest. However, friends and neighbors can offer testimony about a testator's odd behavior or lack of memory to show that he or she lacked the mental ability to draft a valid will. Expert testimony from a physician or psychologist can also be used to show that a testator was insane or working under a delusion so he or she was not capable of drafting a valid will.

Another way to invalidate a will is to claim it was forged by someone else or that the testator was induced to draft the will by fraud.

Forgery or Fraud

Forgery is an uncommon claim in a will contest, although some lawyers have been accused of plots to defraud rightful beneficiaries by forging a will after a client died. Evidence that a will was forged can be circumstantial, such as the naming of unusual beneficiaries or by expert analysis of the testator's signature to determine whether it's valid. In addition, cross-examination of attesting witnesses and testimony from friends and family members who swear that the decedent never drafted a will can be introduced to show that the document offered as a last will is a forgery.[64]

Fraud is another possible basis for contesting a will, but it's a fairly rare claim because fraudulently convincing someone to draft a will is complex and difficult.

Usually claims of fraud are associated with claims of undue influence or lack of capacity to draft a will because these allegations are usually easier to prove in a probate court. There are two types of fraud connected with convincing a testator to draft a defective will: fraud in the inducement, which happens when someone makes a false statement of fact and convinces a testator to draft a will different from what he or she would ordinarily intend, and fraud in the execution, which means someone lied about the actual instrument the testator signed. Fraud in the inducement could happen if someone told the testator a child had said bad things about him or her, inducing the testator to leave that child out of the will. Fraud in the execution would happen if the testator's attorney tells him or her the instrument the testator is signing is a true and correct copy of the will when it's a different document. Fraud in the inducement and execution generally happen to older persons who don't understand what they are doing and trust the wrong person. In these cases, "friends" or "professionals" use the misguided trust of vulnerable older individuals to deceive and defraud them. More often, a will is contested by claiming someone exerted undue influence on an older testator at the time he or she drafted the will.

Undue Influence

Next to lack of capacity, undue influence is the most common claim in a will contest, and often lack of capacity and undue influence are alleged together because they commonly happen at the same time in the drafting of a contested will. Undue influence occurs when someone the testator trusts pressures him or her to draft a will different from what the testator intended. Lack of capacity generally occurs along with undue influence because a person who is older and of weak mind is easier to influence than someone younger and of sound mind. Will contests that allege undue influence often involve older individuals who were taken advantage of by a friend or relative. The claim may be that a housekeeper or a girlfriend unduly influenced an older man to leave his money to them rather than his children. Most cases alleging undue influence concern the naming of unusual beneficiaries such as when the testator leaves most or all of his money to someone outside the family. Examples include wills where the testator left substantial assets to his attorney, doctor, priest, guardian, housekeeper, or a girlfriend rather than giving the estate to his spouse and children.

Influence has to be unreasonable rather than simply the result of natural affection for a caretaker. For example, if a part-time housekeeper has been badgering an old man to leave his money to her, that might constitute undue influence before a probate court. On the other hand, if an old man leaves a tidy sum to someone who affectionately cared for him for years before he died, that is natural and understandable and would not generally be considered undue influence by a probate court. Moreover, if a wife pressured her husband to leave his entire estate to her, that is not usually considered undue influence because a spouse is a natural object of a person's bounty— although her children may object and file a will contest. However, a pretty young girlfriend of an older man who receives everything when he dies is likely to be suspected of undue influence by a probate judge, especially if the testator left nothing to a longtime spouse or children.

Stepchildren sometimes accuse a second wife of undue influence, but unhappy children have contested their father's will when their own mother received everything. Any will can be challenged, but will contests often fail because it's difficult to find convincing evidence that the testator was defrauded, was the victim of undue influence, or lacked capacity to draft his or her will. Partly this is because the level of understanding required to draft a will is fairly low—all the supporter of the will needs to show is that the testator understood in a general way what he or she owned, that the testator could list the individuals who comprise his family and are the natural objects of his bounty, and could correlate assets and family members during the drafting of a will. It is not a difficult task, and one many older persons are capable of competently performing.

Fraud is also difficult to prove. Just because an older testator doesn't give his family all his assets doesn't prove he or she was a victim of fraud or undue influence. It may well be that the testator didn't like some members of his or her family because they snubbed or ignored him or her. Undue influence may be especially difficult to prove if other facts exist to explain the unusual distribution of an estate.

CHAPTER 5

Origin of Trusts and Fiduciary Duties

A modern trust is an agreement in writing between a settlor, who establishes the trust, and a trustee who holds title to trust property and administers the trust for beneficiaries. A trust creates a fiduciary relationship among the trustee, beneficiaries, and settlor. Originally, trusts were informal agreements between settlors and trustees that could not be enforced in English common-law courts. Eventually, English kings established equity courts to hear cases where the trustee refused to comply with the informal agreement and would not return a knight's land when he returned from fighting a crusade. Equity courts eventually developed a body of law protecting the settlor and beneficiaries from dishonest trustees. Many of these court decisions relied on the concept of a fiduciary duty owed by the trustee to the settlor and beneficiaries of a trust. A fiduciary duty demands a high degree of honesty and candor on the part of the trustee to treat the settlor and beneficiaries fairly and prudently—a trustee must place the interests of the settlor and beneficiaries above his own.[65]

In most trusts, there are three roles: a settlor, a trustee, and beneficiaries. In the case of a living trust, the settlor, trustee, and beneficiary are generally the same person (the settlor). The purpose of a living trust is to avoid the time, expense, and publicity of probating a will by automatically distributing trust assets to a widow, a minor, or disabled individuals after the settlor dies. Property in a living trust passes to named successor beneficiaries (usually the surviving spouse and children) when the settlor/trustee/beneficiary passes away without any need for a probate proceeding. Moreover, the settlor can keep personal assets private after death because there is no need to file an inventory and appraisement with the probate court as is required with a will.

Origin of Trusts

The English law of trusts was developed by courts of equity to correct injustices in the common law concerning the ownership of land. Early English common law regarded rights to land as indivisible, meaning that the person who held legal title to land was automatically entitled to the use and enjoyment of profits from that land. When a common-law court was confronted with a case where a knight, who left on a crusade and entrusted his land to a trustee or manager, returned and asked the trustee to give him back his land, but the trustee refused to honor his original agreement, the common-law court could not look beyond the legal title to the land in deciding who actually owned the real estate.[66] Common-law courts were forced to rule that the trustee owned the land because he held title, and there was no way to introduce evidence in a common-law court about the prior agreement between the trustee and the crusading knight. To correct this injustice, English kings established and maintained equity courts to determine ownership of land in these cases on the basis of fairness rather than rigid common-law rules. Equity judges ruled that legal title to land could be separated from equitable use and enjoyment of the land, and the result was the legal doctrine of trusts.[67]

Purpose of a Trust

Trusts evolved to deal with the rigid restrictions English common law placed on the ownership and conveyance of land, to avoid the many fees kings levied on feudal land, and to allow the Catholic Church to use and enjoy land bequeathed to it. We have already seen how trusts helped knights returning from the crusades reclaim their land. After the Norman Conquest of England, King William gave land to his nobles in feudal tenure. In return, he was entitled to a cash payment when land descended from a father to his son, when a wardship needed to be established because the inheritor of land was a minor, on the marriage of a daughter of the lord, the knighting of his eldest son, or when a lord was captured and held for ransom during war. These and other financial burdens fell on the feudal landholder and they could be onerous if the king was unreasonable or actively fighting a war. By establishing a trust and giving legal title to a trustee, the feudal landholder hoped to escape these burdens on his land and at the same time gain the right to transfer the land during his lifetime to someone outside his immediate family or gift the land by will at his death to someone other than his eldest son.[68] Finally, because the Catholic Church could not own land, it was forced to appoint trustees to hold title to the land and pay taxes to the king so the church could enjoy the use of the land bequeathed to it.

It took a long time for courts to recognize the doctrine of trusts because it required separating the legal title to land from the use and enjoyment of the land, and that was not possible under existing English common law. Today, trusts can be created in various ways.

Creation and Operation of Trusts

Trusts can be created by operation of law, through a will, or by means of a written document signed by the trustee and the settlor describing the trust property; naming the trustee, settlor, and beneficiaries; and setting out the trust terms. The trust document describes management of the assets, disposition of trust holdings, and the rights and duties of the parties. The trustee holds legal title to the trust property and manages, invests, and distributes assets for the support, maintenance, education, and health of beneficiaries. Often a trustee is given discretion to distribute funds according to the beneficiary's needs, typical standard of living, and the availability of trust income. The trustee may be given the right to invade the principal of a trust to pay expenses of a beneficiary or restricted to distributing only income from the trust.[69]

The earliest courts to enforce the duty of a trustee to hold title to land and pass it on to the ultimate beneficiary named in the landowner's will were ecclesiastical courts, but later the king's chancery courts stepped in to settle disputes between church and civil courts and enforce informal agreements on the ownership and use of land.

Ecclesiastical Courts

English law forbade religious corporations from owning land under the Mortmain Acts, passed by Edward I in 1279 and 1290. These laws were intended to preserve the right of the English crown to collect revenue from land by preventing it from passing into the hands of the Church, which was exempt from taxes. *Mortmain* was derived from Norman French and means "dead hand."[70] Also, because many religious orders take vows of poverty, owning land was inconsistent with living a simple clerical life. The Catholic Church avoided restrictions placed on land ownership under the Mortmain Actsby gifting the land to a layman trustee for use by the church. By establishing a trust and giving legal title to church land to a trustee, the king could collect taxes from the layman trustee, and the religious orders were able to manage the property and enjoy the benefits of income from land without breaking the law by holding legal title to the land themselves. Trusts were developed by ecclesiastical courts so the Church could enjoy revenues from lands gifted to it by dying Catholics without holding legal title to the land.

Trusts also developed through equity court rulings that avoided the rigid rules of English common law relating to the ownership and use of real property when crusading knights returned from their quest to find that their trustee refused to return the knights' land to him. Trust law developed gradually from decisions by ecclesiastical and chancery courts to enforce informal agreements between a manager or trustee who held legal title to land and an owner who asked the trustee to hold the land while he was away on a crusade and return the property when the original owner returned.[71] Because some dishonest trustees were not honoring their agreements to return entrusted land to its rightful owner, and common-law courts could not enforce these agreements, the king ordered his chancellor to intervene and administer justice to his knights, and later the Church, on the basis of fairness rather than rigid common-law rules. The king did not want a dishonest trustee benefiting from fraud and claiming a knight's land because the trustee held legal title, and the common law could not look beyond who held title to the land to decide the real owner. Equity courts enforced the informal agreement between a crusader or the Church and a trustee and forced the trustee to return the land to its rightful owner.

Early equity court decisions supported the doctrine that legal title to land and beneficial use of the same land could be separated, meaning that a trustee could hold legal title to land for a beneficiary who could enjoy the income or use of the land, and the trust agreement could be enforced in a court of equity. Ancient Roman law allowed trusts created by will, but these Roman trusts operated only after the testator's death (testamentary trusts) and didn't allow the creation of a trust during the lifetime of the individual (living trust). Consequently, English and American courts had to develop new legal doctrines to deal with the situation where an owner entrusted land to a trustee or manager to be held for the benefit of another while the settlor was living. Equity courts ruled that a trustee could hold legal title to land for the use and enjoyment of beneficiaries and that title and use of land could be separated.

During the reign of King Edward, another court system developed in addition to church and common-law courts—the chancery court.

Chancery Courts

The lord chancellor, who was the king's representative, heard disputes involving informal agreements between crusading knights or the Roman Catholic Church and trustees who refused to honor their bargains to hold the knights' or church's land in trust for their use. The chancery courts decided that the person who held legal title to land (a trustee) could be different from the person who enjoyed use of the land (a beneficiary), and the chancery court would enforce these informal trust agreements by invoking the doctrine of fiduciary duty.[72] Chancery courts, under authority of the king's council, decided these cases on the basis of "fairness" rather than following the strict requirements of English common law.

Chancery courts operated under the control and direction of the lord chancellor as keeper of the king's conscience and applied flexible rules of procedure and the equitable doctrine of "fairness" in reaching their decisions. Chancery courts were administrative bodies concerned with equity rather than judicial courts required to interpret and enforce English common law, so they followed equity rules and different legal procedures, and they didn't adhere to rigid and inflexible common-law rules that disallowed any suit that didn't fit into preexisting case law. The court of chancery had a wider purpose, flexible procedures, and more remedies than law courts. Because the chancery court was a direct representative of the king, it could overrule common-law courts and base their rulings on "fairness." The chancery court's jurisdiction was unlimited, holding executive, judicial, and legislative powers derived directly from the king, who held absolute power.[73]

Moreover, a chancery court could call on remedies other than money damages, including specific performance (requiring a defendant to fulfill the exact terms of his or her contract) and injunctions (requiring a defendant to stop doing something unlawful). The English court of chancery grew in power and authority until the fifteenth century, when it became a separate judicial body composed of judges and clerks who heard cases and made decisions based on equitable principles rather than the strict rules of common law.[74]

Chancery courts developed and operated in parallel with common-law and church courts for centuries in England. English common-law courts didn't recognize a knight's claim for the return of his property when he finished a crusade; instead, common law judges follow the strict rules of English law and held that a manager or trustee had no duty to return the land to the knight because English common law didn't allow the separation of legal and equitable title in land. The king decided it was unconscionable for a trustee to retain ownership of land a knight had entrusted to him while the knight fought in a crusade, so he instructed his chancellor to handle these cases equitably. Rulings by the court of chancery established the legal principal that a trustee only held legal title to land in trust (as a trustee) for the use and enjoyment of the knight when he returned from the crusades—at which time the trustee was obligated to return legal title to the knight, and the chancery court would enforce the trust agreement.

Chancery courts accumulated a large staff of clerks controlled by the master of the rolls, who had the power to hear cases and borrow judges from law courts as needed. The chancery court charged fees to hear cases and earned funds for the king by dispensing equitable justice. At first the court of chancery heard mostly disputes involving verbal contracts, land title disputes, and matters involving trustees who were not honoring their informal agreements with settlors. The chancery court also handled debt contracts where one party was poor and could not repay the debt, allowing some to avoid debtor's prison. Most important for our purpose, chancery courts enforced agreements between trustees and knights or the Roman Catholic Church concerning the separation of legal title to land and the equitable use and enjoyment of the land.

After centuries of growth in power and influence, chancery courts came to be resented by the English nobility, however.

Chancery Court Reforms

As the chancery court's jurisdiction and influence grew, the English nobility became concerned that the king and his staff were usurping too many of their rights and powers. During the English Civil War (1642–51), the chancery court was criticized for its equitable rules and procedures compared with common-law courts. In 1649, Parliament passed statutes reforming the chancery court, requiring that attorneys bring pleas rather than allowing defendants to represent themselves, and scheduling cases to be heard in the order they were filed rather than giving priority to persons with political power or social influence.[75] Parliament also fixed the fees chancery courts could charge for hearing a case. Many chancery court judges were removed by Cromwell's administration during the English Civil War, but most were returned to their posts after the English Restoration.

In addition to reforming the chancery courts, Parliament also passed laws modernizing the common law courts, allowing appeals from lower court rulings when there was uncertainty about whether proper procedures and rules of evidence had been followed. As a result of these reforms, chancery courts were no longer concerned with correcting errors occurring in law courts and instead focused on administrative duties and protecting the rights of trust beneficiaries (similar to modern statutory probate courts).

Eventually, Parliament decided to combine common-law and chancery courts into a single judicial system.

Common-Law and Chancery Courts

Support for uniting common-law and chancery courts grew during the 1850s in response to pressure from lawyers working in common-law courts who didn't like the equitable procedures used in chancery courts. The process of combining the two court systems began with the passage of the Common Law Procedures Act in 1854 and the Chancery Amendment Act of 1858, which gave both court systems the right to apply a full range of remedies to any case before them. Next, the County Courts Act of 1865 gave law courts authority to use equitable procedures, so there was basically no remaining difference between law courts and chancery courts. Finally, Parliament combined the two court systems by giving law courts the right to hear evidence and decide all trial cases and assigning the right of appeal to an equitable court of appeals (the old chancery courts).

The doctrine of trusts developed from equitable court rulings upholding informal agreements between crusading knights or the Catholic Church and trustees to hold land for the equitable use of the knights or church. These agreements could not be enforced in English common-law courts if a trustee didn't adhere to the bargain, because English common law didn't recognize the separation of legal title from the equitable use of land in medieval times.[76] Equity court decisions gradually developed a body of law protecting the settlor and beneficiary from a dishonest trustee, creating the English doctrine of trusts. These equity court decisions relied on the concept of fiduciary duty owed by a trustee to the settlor and beneficiaries of the trust to enforce the agreement. The fiduciary relationship between a trustee and the settlor and beneficiaries demands a high degree of honesty and candor on the part of the trustee to treat the settlor and beneficiaries fairly and prudently, and trustees must place the interests of the settlor and beneficiaries above their own.[77]

The idea of a fiduciary duty developed in ancient contract law.

Contract Law

The concept of fiduciary duty had been around for centuries prior to the development of trusts in the form of duties owed in contract law between a merchant and his agent and in religious rules for living— "do unto to others as you would have them do unto you." In its most basic form, a fiduciary duty arises when one person relies on another to do a task or service for him or her as an agent. The concept of a fiduciary duty required an agent to place the interests of his principal above his own and originally developed within the ancient law of contracts. For example, in an action of account, landholders sued their rent collectors, and the courts enforced the contact by making the rent collector give an accounting and pay any amounts due the landowner based on the fiduciary duty owed the landowner by his rent collector.

English courts borrowed the concept of fiduciary duty from ancient contract law and first applied it to cases involving agents and principals.

Fiduciary Duty

English equity courts borrowed the idea of fiduciary duty from ancient Mesopotamian commercial and contract law. The legal doctrine of a fiduciary was first used by English common-law judges to enforce duties owed by an agent to a merchant who gave him funds to purchase goods in another city and have them delivered to the merchant's home base. Later, courts of equity applied the concept of fiduciary duty to trustees who owed a duty to beneficiaries when holding legal title to trust property for the benefit of others.

A fiduciary duty owed by one person to another was present in the Hammurabi Code published during the seventeenth century BC.[78] The concept of agency and fiduciary duty developed in ancient Mesopotamia to handle situations where a merchant gave another person, called an agent, money to use for travel, investment, or the purchase of goods for his principal. Courts used the doctrine of fiduciary duty to hold the agent accountable to his principal for the funds.

Other early examples of fiduciary duty can be found in the Bible and Greek writings.

The Bible

The Bible contains several examples of fiduciary duty. In *The Republic*, Plato outlined the duties a philosopher king owed his subjects, and these were similar to modern ideas of fiduciary duty. The ancient Romans used the term *fiduciary* in their laws and defined it to mean a person having a duty to others to place their interests above his own—analogous to the modern duties of a trustee or agent. The concept of fiduciary duty was so important that four chapters of the Magna Charta listed remedies for heirs against guardians for withholding or wasting their inheritance.[79]

Fiduciary duties were routinely enforced by common-law courts in cases of contract law, but not in the case of trust agreements.

Common-Law Courts

Common-law courts enforced an agent's fiduciary duty to account for funds advanced by a principal to trade on his account under the law of contacts. Agents who refused to produce an accounting of their principal's funds were sent to prison until they either accounted for the funds or returned the money their principals had given them. The action of waste in a wardship was also based on the enforcement of a fiduciary duty of a guardian to account for the profits of his ward's land. The duties of a fiduciary included loyalty, care, and prudence.

Definition of Fiduciary

Current fiduciary duties in English and American law exceed those developed in early English common law, but the beginnings of legal fiduciary duties are clearly visible as early at the thirteenth century in England. Benjamin Cardozo wrote the most cited words defining the duties of a fiduciary: "Many forms of conduct permissible in a workaday world for those acting at arm's length, are forbidden to those bound by fiduciary ties. A trustee is held to something stricter than the morals of the marketplace. Not honesty alone, but the punctilio of an honor the most sensitive, is then the standard of behavior."[80]

English and American trust law developed out of the earlier English concept of use.

The Doctrine of Uses

The doctrine of uses (which eventually became the law of trusts) was a legal concept developed to handle a situation where two parties agreed that legal title to property would be held by one person, whose name would appear on a deed to land, but a different actual state of affairs would be given effect in the real world—the land was actually held for the use, enjoyment, or benefit of others called the beneficiaries. The trustee, as he or she came to be called, would hold legal title to property and owe a fiduciary duty to carry out the terms of the trust agreement for the "use and enjoyment" of beneficiaries.[81] One purpose of uses was to allow the Catholic Church to enjoy income from lands willed to it by Catholics when they died. Holding church land in trust was necessary because it was illegal for the church to own land directly because it paid no taxes to the king.

Enforcement of Fiduciary Duties

The common law's inability to enforce trusts and fiduciary duties was most harmful in the case of real property law, but this inability to enforce uses also damaged the enforcement of debt instruments. For example, when someone signed and sealed a bond promising to pay a debt, and then paid the debt, the debtor expected his creditor to destroy the signed bond because the debt had been paid. However, if a creditor didn't destroy the signed bond, he could take the bond into a common-law court, sue the debtor, and collect a second time on the same sealed debt bond because the common-law court would not hear evidence that the debtor had already paid the loan. Under the law existing at the time, a common-law court could only consider the signed and sealed bond as evidence that a debt was owed, and it would force the debtor to pay a second time.

This outcome was so obviously unjust that the king directed courts of chancery to hear these cases on the basis of fairness rather than the common law and allowed the equity courts to hear evidence that the debt had already been paid. Only in a court of equity could a debtor get relief by being able to prove he had already paid the debt. The common law gained a reputation as a complex set of rigid rules used by unscrupulous persons and attorneys to defraud their more trusting neighbors. Once the concept of uses was firmly established and enforced in equity courts, it was expanded into other areas.

Trusts and Feudal Tenure

Other cases where the concept of uses was applied involved a feudal landholder who wanted to avoid the onerous fees owed the king when land passed to his son, when his daughter married, when his son was knighted, or when he was captured and needed to be ransomed. A feudal landholder could not do that under the English law of primogeniture governing feudal lands. Moreover, if an heir of a feudal landholder was under the age of twenty-one years when his father died, he became a ward of the king, who received the profits from the ward's land as compensation for overseeing the property until the ward attained majority. However, these lucrative rights were only available if the land was inherited after the death of the prior owner. If the landholder gave his land away during his lifetime (or placed the land in a trust), the king's right of wardship was not available because a trustee was already in place to manage the property, and income from the land could accrue to the ward rather than the king. English lawyers and lords believed the concept of uses would help them avoid onerous fees on tenured land.

To avoid the high costs imposed on the inheritance of land by feudal tenure, lords who held feudal land developed the practice of deeding real property to a group of friends, with the understanding that they would transfer title to the land back to a person (other than the owner's firstborn son), who was named in the original landholder's will. This arrangement allowed the landholder to avoid passing all his land to his eldest son and also escape the costs of wardship if his son was under the age of twenty-one when he died. Thus, by means of what came to be called a *use* in English common law, a landholder could avoid taxes due his king when he died and pass some of his property to younger sons. However, the beneficiary of a use had no protection at common law if the feudal landholder's friends didn't live up to their agreement with his father and breached their fiduciary duty by keeping title to his land rather than passing title on to the beneficiary named in the original landholder's will. Gradually, the doctrine of uses developed through equity court decisions enforcing these informal agreements into the law of trusts.

The early development of trust law produced two different types, active and passive.[82]

Types of Trusts

Two types of trusts developed from expansion of the doctrine of uses—special active trusts and general passive trusts. Ecclesiastical courts expanded the legal doctrine of use to allow a layman to hold legal title to the land in trust (but with no administrative or management obligations other than to pay taxes) for the benefit of a religious order. In addition, uses were expanded to allow flexibility in the conveying of land to a trust during an owner's lifetime and to gain the power to transfer title to property automatically on the death of the settlor who formed the trust. Uses developed into what was called a passive trust that required the trustee to hold legal title to the land while allowing the beneficiary to manage the land and enjoy any income and other benefits from the property. Trustees of passive uses had no responsibility to administer or manage the real property for the beneficiary. Passive trusts served to separate legal and equitable title to land so a layman could hold legal title to the land and pay taxes to the king, but the Church would manage the property and enjoy income from the land without breaking the law by holding legal title to land, which was prohibited because the Church paid no taxes to the king.

On the other hand, if a trustee held legal title to property in trust and also assumed active management of the land, the arrangement was called an active or special trust. For example, if A conveyed land to B and instructed B to manage the land and pay the profits to C, B was an active or special trustee and owed a fiduciary duty to C to manage the property, collect rents, and pay profits to beneficiary C.

Originally, trusts modeled on the doctrine of uses were purely voluntary and could not be enforced in courts of law. If a trustee denied he held title to land for the benefit of another, the beneficiary had no legal remedy in a court of common law. In contrast, fiduciary duties concerning money and chattels were enforced in common-law courts by an action of account. Equity courts, which could order specific performance of the trusteeship rather than simply money damages, began hearing these cases and enforcing the informal agreement so a beneficiary could receive his land from the dishonest trustee. To clarify the law of trusts and give them a solid legal foundation, Parliament passed the Statute of Uses in 1535.[83]

The Statute of Uses

King Henry VIII pressured Parliament to pass the Statute of Uses to curb the avoidance of taxes by the Catholic Church and to stop landowners from evading expenses incurred by a feudal landholder when he died, his daughters married, or his sons were knighted. The Statute of Uses also reinstated the old English rule of primogeniture where the firstborn son inherited all a lord's land and titles.[84] However, the Statute of Uses didn't have its intended effect because common-law courts narrowly interpreted the wording contained in the Statute of Uses. As a result, equitable uses continued to exist and eventually formed the legal doctrine of trusts. The Statute of Uses, passed in 1535, was intended to give a beneficiary real property to hold in fee simple rather than in trust, but the statute didn't have that effect.

Equitable interests, which were supposed to be outlawed by the Statute of Uses, continued to exist for generations because common-law courts strictly interpreted the exact words in the Statute of Uses and continued to apply uses to personal property because the statute only mentioned real property. Also, because the statute said it applied only to land where title was seized (which meant legal possession of the land free from feudal tenure), law courts held that only freehold estates were controlled by the Statute of Uses—whereas feudal land was exempt from the statute. In addition, land held for life or a term of years was not affected by the Statute of Uses, and neither was an active trust. Only passive trusts were subject to the Statute of Uses according to narrow common-law court interpretations of the statute.

An active trust requires the administrator or trustee to hold legal title to the land, manage it, and pay the income to a beneficiary. If A conveyed land to B to hold and manage for the benefit of C and his heirs, that was an active trust, and the Statute of Uses had no effect on that trust arrangement because common-law courts ruled that only passive trusts were covered by the statute. As a result of these narrow interpretations of the Statute of Uses by common-law courts, many uses were exempted from the statute, even though Parliament had originally intended to abolish all uses. To avoid confusion, the chancery court changed the title of these equitable interests unaffected by the Statute of Uses to trusts and continued to enforce their terms.

The English law of trusts was codified in 1925 by a series of trust acts, and American trust doctrine developed along similar lines.

American Trust Law

American courts borrowed the idea of a fiduciary duty (a legal concept developed in contract law to deal with the duties an agent owed to his principal) from English common law and applied it to the relationship between a trustee and a beneficiary. The trustee's fiduciary duty was to administer and distribute trust property for the enjoyment of named beneficiaries in a fair and prudent manner without regard to the trustee's personal interests.[85] American trust law gave beneficiaries the right to sue in civil court to force the trustee to administer the property in accordance with the terms of the trust or be removed, ordered to pay money damages, and be replaced by a new trustee who would follow the terms of the trust instrument.

In America, it's possible to create trusts that are effective during the lifetime of the settlor (living trusts) as well as trusts that become effective on the death of the settlor (testamentary trusts). In the case of a living trust, the settlor drafts a document appointing himself as trustee to manage and administer the trust property for his own benefit during the settlor's lifetime and names a successor trustee to administer trust property for the use and enjoyment of named beneficiaries after the settlor's death. Trustees have a fiduciary duty to carry out the terms of the trust without self-interest. A trustee must manage, invest, and distribute the trust property according to the terms of the trust, and if he or she does not, the trustee is in breach of a fiduciary duty and can be held liable for damages and removed as trustee.

The settlor of a trust is the person who originally creates the trust and transfers property into it. Most modern living trusts name the settlor as primary trustee during his or her lifetime and one or more successor trustees to manage and distribute the trust property after the death of the settlor. The major goal of establishing a living trust is to transfer property automatically to named beneficiaries when the settlor dies and allow the transfer without the necessity of probating a will. The American Law Institute released its Restatement of the American Law of Trusts in 1935 and revised the Restatement of Trusts in 1957.

CHAPTER 6

Wills of Famous People

You can learn a lot about famous people by reading their last will and testament. Many famous people left written wills, including all American presidents except Abraham Lincoln. Lincoln was an accomplished lawyer and the only president who didn't leave a will. It's not surprising Lincoln didn't leave a will—he was exceptionally busy the last years of his life managing the war against the Confederacy, and immediately after the war ended, he was assassinated.

We begin our review with a reconstructed will drafted by Alexander the Great around 323 BC.

Alexander the Great.[86]

David Grant, an English expert on Alexander the Great, believes the last chapter of an ancient manuscript known as the "Alexander Romance" contains details of Alexander's last will. Grant argues that Alexander's last will and testament was suppressed because his generals didn't want Alexander's "half-breed sons" ruling his empire. Instead of allowing a hereditary succession based on Alexander's will, his generals suppressed the true will, forged another, and fought each other for power. Grant asserts that Alexander's last will named his sons Alexander IV and Heracles as his successors, but his generals issued a fake one which stated that the ruler of Alexander's lands would be "the strongest of them." His generals started a civil war that tore Alexander's empire apart. Would history have been different if Alexander's original will had been followed? Perhaps, but we shall never know.

We turn next to Julius Caesar's last will.

Julius Caesar.[87]

A copy of Caesar's last will and testament has not survived, but we know the circumstances surrounding his death on March 15, 44 BC. We can infer the basic terms of Caesar's will from records of Marc Antony's reading of it to the people of Rome. Caesar left his gardens in Rome to the city for a park and gave what was described by Marc Antony as "a large amount of money" to every citizen of Rome. Caesar left seventy-five drachmas; one drachma contained approximately 4.3 ounces of silver, worth around $75 today. Thus, Caesar gifted the modern equivalent of approximately $5,500 to every inhabitant of Rome. He was certainly a wealthy and powerful man when he died. Caesar's body was burned in the forum before a large crowd of Roman citizens, who saw his bloody cloak and heard that they would each receive a substantial sum of money from his estate when Marc Antony delivered his funeral oration for Caesar and turned Roman citizens against his murderers.

In his will, Caesar adopted Octavian as heir to his title, power, and residual estate. Ironically, Decimus Brutus, one of Caesar's murderers, was named as an alternate adopted son and heir in Caesar's will, if Octavian didn't survive Caesar. By adopting Octavian in his will, Caesar effectively named him the first Emperor of Rome and left him three-fourths of an enormous estate. As we know from history, Octavian was forced to defend his claim to the Roman throne by fighting and winning a civil war against Marc Antony and Cleopatra.

The next will we examine was drafted by King Henry VIII of England.

Henry VIII.[88] King Henry signed his last will on December 30, 1546, transferring royal authority to his young son Prince Edward when he died. Henry repented in his will and resolved never to return to his old ways, bequeathed his soul to God, and directed that his body be laid in the choir of the college in Windsor, midway between the stalls and the high altar with the bones of his wife, Queen Jane. He requested that his executors arrange a service for the dead at a suitable place and have his body buried according to his instructions. Henry gave land to St. George's College so priests would say mass at the altar where he was buried.

Henry VIII directed in his will that the crown of England shall go to Prince Edward and the heirs of his body. In default, it went to Henry's children by his present wife Queen Catherine, or any future wife. In default, it went to his daughter Mary and the heirs of her body, upon condition that she shall not marry without the written and sealed consent of a majority of the surviving members of the Privy Council appointed by Henry VIII. In default, it went to his daughter Elizabeth under the same conditions. Henry appointed fifteen English lords to be his executors and members of the Privy Council while Prince Edward was a minor (Edward was nine when his father, Henry VIII, died). Henry directed that the Privy Counsel and executors take all actions by a majority of them rather than individually. He also asked that all his legal debts should be paid, although he knew of none.

Henry named his son Prince Edward to the thrones of England and Ireland and to the title of France, and he gave Edward his plate, household furniture and fixtures, artillery, ordinance, ships, money, and jewels. He charged his son to be ruled by the Privy Council until he was eighteen years of age. Henry gave Mary and Elizabeth ten thousand pounds each. He instructed his executors to give each of them more at their discretion and distribute three thousand pounds annually to each of them for living expenses. Henry made a number of smaller bequeaths to his councilors and servants.

We turn next to the famous playwright, William Shakespeare, who drafted his will on March 25, 1616.

William Shakespeare.[89]

Shakespeare's last will and testament contains important information about his life, family, professional associates, and the property he owned when he died. The will was probably drafted by a clerk in his attorney's office because it shows none of the style characteristic of the great poet and playwright. Shakespeare signed each of the three pages of his will in his own hand, and experts have noted that each signature is different, perhaps because he was ill when he signed the document and was in bed.

Shakespeare left most of his property to his daughters, Susanne Hall and Judith Quiney. He also gifted money to his sister Joan Hart and her three sons, as well as a silver plate to his granddaughter Elizabeth Hall. Shakespeare bequeathed a large silver bowl to his daughter Judith, a sword to Thomas Combe, and his second-best bed to his wife. Experts have noted the gift of his second-best bed to his wife, Anne Hathaway, wondering if that bequest suggested they were estranged. Anne is mentioned nowhere else in his will, so their marital relationship is puzzling at best. Shakespeare's wife would have received one-third of his estate automatically according to English law, so there was no need for him to mention the second-best bed in his will unless he had a personal reason for doing it.

Shakespeare's will was attested by Francis Collins (his attorney) and four friends. Shakespeare named his daughter Susanne Hall and her husband John Hall as executors of his estate. Shakespeare died on April 23, 1616, and his will was probated on June 22, 1616. The inventory of his goods has been lost, probably in the Great Fire of London in 1666. Shakespeare's estate consisted of land, cash, four houses, and personal property worth under one thousand pounds in total. Shakespeare's original last will and testament is stored at the National Archives in Kew, England.

Next, we move forward to early America and the will of our first president, George Washington.

George Washington.[90]

Washington drafted two versions of his last will and testament and decided which one he wanted to be effective while he was on his deathbed. He asked his wife, Martha, to burn the discarded will and safeguard the other, which is currently preserved at Mount Vernon, his family home. At his death on December 14, 1799, Washington owned vast sections of wilderness land in the West; improved lots in Washington D.C. and Alexandria, Virginia; his home and surrounding land at Mount Vernon; and large tracts of semi-improved land in Ohio, Maryland, Pennsylvania, and New York.

Washington directed that all his debts, although minor, be paid from his estate by his executor. His primary goal was to care for his wife, and he directed his executor to make certain she was supported throughout the remainder of her life from income generated by his estate. Washington directed, in his handwritten will, that Martha receive the "use, profit, and benefit of my whole estate, real and personal, for the term of her natural life." At Martha's death, Washington's entire remaining estate was to be divided among a group of listed beneficiaries by his executors.

Washington disposed of some assets for charitable purposes in his will, and he was generous with his relatives, forgiving debts owed by his brother Samuel's estate, loans to his brother's sons, and debts owed by Martha's brother. Washington freed all the slaves he owned after Martha's death. He provided financial support for young and old freed slaves and stipulated in his will that young freed slaves be taught to read and write and receive training in a useful occupation. Washington prohibited the sale or transportation of his slaves from Virginia and ordered his executors to take care of them according to his instructions. Washington wanted to free Martha's slaves after her death, but he couldn't because they were owned by her in dower, and he was powerless to free them. Washington freed his mulatto slave William Lee (his personal servant for years) and gave him a stipend of thirty dollars annually so long as William Lee should live.

Washington gifted, in trust, four thousand dollars to support a school for orphans and to establish a university in Washington D.C., although the university never opened. He also gave shares in the James River Company to Liberty Hall Academy, which later became Washington and Lee University in Lexington, Virginia. Washington gave all his civil and military administrative papers to his nephew, Bushrod Washington, for safekeeping. Washington gifted a gold-headed cane given him by Ben Franklin to his brother Charles Washington, and he gave Bushrod Washington his home at Mount Vernon and a substantial parcel of land around it, described in detail in the will. Washington gave his lands east of Little Hunting Creek to George Fayette Washington and Lawrence (Charles) Washington, to be divided equitably between them. He also gave a large tract of land to Martha's children. Washington directed that the remainder of his estate not already described and gifted be sold and divided equally into twenty-three parts and given to a list of specifically named beneficiaries at his death.

Washington signed and sealed his will on July 9, 1799. His will was presented for probate on January 10, 1800, and the court appointed a set of appraisers to value his assets at Mount Vernon. Washington's estate was closed on June 21, 1847.

Next, we move to France and review the will of Napoleon Bonaparte.

Napoleon Bonaparte.[91]

Napoleon drafted his last will and testament in his own hand on April 15, 1821, and added five codicils later that month. Napoleon stated he died in the Apostolical Roman religion and requested in his last will that his ashes be scattered on the banks of the Seine among the people of France. He asked his wife, Maria Louisa, to watch over his son, and he asked his son to follow the motto "Everything for the French People." Napoleon alleged that he was being assassinated by the English oligarchy. Napoleon gave his personal effects to his son Napoleon Francois Joseph Charles Bonaparte.

Napoleon gifted two million francs to Count Montholon, one of his generals and a devoted supporter, as reward for his loyalty. Napoleon also gave several monetary bequests to other listed beneficiaries. He directed that all these sums should be paid from a six-million-franc account deposited at a Paris bank in 1815 at 5 percent interest. Napoleon also stipulated in his will that any funds remaining in that account, after paying the named beneficiaries, be distributed among the French soldiers wounded at the battle of Waterloo and among the officers and soldiers of the battalion on the isle of Elba. He directed that if these individuals had already died, then the gifts should go to their widows and orphans.

Napoleon estimated that his residual estate should be worth around two hundred million francs at his death. He gave half these funds to the surviving officers and soldiers of the French army who fought from 1792 to 1815 for the glory of France, to be distributed proportionally to their service in the army during that interval. He donated the other half of his residual estate to the various districts of France. Napoleon signed and dated his will on April 15, 1821, and annexed several lists to the will.

On April 16, 1821, Napoleon wrote two codicils to his will. Codicil one reiterated that his ashes be scattered on the banks of the Seine and gave his silver, jewels, plate, and more to Counts Bertrand and Monotholon and to Marchand. Codicil two explained that he gave everything he owned on St. Helena to the counts in order to keep his property out of the hands of the British. Napoleon directed that the funds derived from his personal property on St. Helena be distributed to the domestics who served him on the island during his incarceration.

On April 24, 1821, Napoleon drafted additional codicils to his will. Codicil three directed that two million francs on deposit in Italy be administered by his son Eugene Napoleon and given to his faithful servants. Napoleon drafted another codicil directing that his jewels be sold and used to discharge personal obligations to certain named individuals. In a fourth codicil to his will, Napoleon gave various sums to the officers of the artillery school at Auxonne, where he had attended classes when he had been stationed in the region. Napoleon also bequeathed ten thousand francs to Subaltern Officer Cantillon, who was tried for trying to assassinate Lord Wellington. In his last codicil, Napoleon forgave his wife, Maria Louisa, a two-million-franc debt and recommended that she protect his faithful servants.

The next will we examine was drafted by Thomas Jefferson in his own hand on March 16, 1826.

Thomas Jefferson.[92]

Jefferson drafted his holographic will of two pages and signed both of them. A day later, he drafted a codicil. Jefferson gave his grandson Francis Eppes all the lands at Poplar Forest bounded by various creeks and public roads described in his will. He subjected all his other property to the payment of any debts remaining at his death.

Because his son-in-law Thomas Mann Randolph was insolvent, Jefferson left the remainder of his estate and the estate of his deceased wife to his grandson Thomas J. Randolph by deed of settlement (a legal agreement between parties) to be held in trust for the sole benefit of his daughter, Martha Randolph, and her heirs. Jefferson required no security for the administration of his estate, and he asked that his personal possessions not be inventoried and appraised. Jefferson appointed Thomas J. Randolph as his primary executor and named Nicholas P. Trist and Alexander Garrett as successor executors and trustees.

In a codicil to his will, Jefferson requested that his daughter, Martha Randolph, take care of his sister, Ann S. Marks, for the remainder of her life. Jefferson gave his friend, James Madison, a gold-mounted walking staff of animal horn. He gave the University of Virginia, which he founded, his extensive library. Jefferson gave a silver watch to his grandson Thomas Jefferson Randolph, explaining that it was better than his gold one. Jefferson gave a gold watch to each of his grandchildren to be delivered when each grandson reached twenty-one years of age and each granddaughter reached sixteen years of age. Jefferson freed his slave and servant Burwell in his will and gave him the sum of three hundred dollars. Jefferson also freed John Hemings and Joe Fosset one year after his death. He specified that his estate should build a "comfortable" log cabin for each of the freed slaves. Jefferson gave John Hemings the services of two slaves, Madison and Eston Hemings, until they reached twenty-one years of age, when they were to be freed. Jefferson asked the Virginia legislature to confirm these bequests of freedom and allow the freed slaves to remain in Virginia.

Jefferson's last will was probated in Albemarle County Court on August 7, 1826, approximately four months after he signed the documents.

Our next famous will was drafted by Robert E. Lee.

Robert E. Lee.[93]

On August 31, 1846, Lee drafted a holographic will revoking all prior wills. He asked that all his debts be punctually and speedily paid, and he gave the balance of his estate to his wife, Mary Custis Lee, for the term of her natural life for her support and the care and education of their children. At the time his will was written, Lee had an estate valued at $38,750. Following his wife's death, Lee specified that his estate be divided among his children "in such portion to each as their situations and necessities in life may require and as may be designated by her" (his wife). Lee specifically noted in his will that because his daughter, Ann Carter, received an injury to one of her eyes, she might be in more need than the other children and should be considered appropriately. He appointed his wife and his son, George Washington Custis Lee, as executrix and executor of his estate. Lee signed the will in his own hand, affixed his seal, and had it witnessed by an army captain of engineers and a civilian working and living on the post where Lee was serving.

Lee added a codicil to his will freeing his slave Nancy and her children at the White House, New Kent, as soon as it could be done to their advantage. His codicil also listed assets Lee owned at the time, including an undivided third part of a tract of land given him by his mother that he was selling for $2,500. Lee's codicil also listed property in Hardy, Virginia, belonging to the estate of his father, a share of the claim of property leased to the government by his father at Harper's Ferry, and a third of two hundred acres of land in Fairfax County, Virginia.

The original handwritten will was produced in court on November 7, 1870, and proved by the oaths of Governor J. Letcher and Colonel William Allen to be in Lee's handwriting. Lee's wife and son acknowledged a bond of one hundred thousand dollars according to the law of Virginia. Lee's wife did not want to qualify as executrix, and the task was assumed by Lee's son George Washington Custis Lee. The total Lee estate was estimated to be less than fifty thousand dollars, a duty stamp of one dollar was paid on the executor's bond, and fifty dollars in state tax was assessed.

Next, we describe the disposition of Abraham Lincoln's estate, who died intestate.

Abraham Lincoln.[94]

Because Lincoln didn't leave a will, his estate was distributed according to the intestate laws of Illinois. Lincoln's estate was administered through the Illinois probate process, which had three steps. First, all assets not in Lincoln's estate, such as property owned jointly with right of survivorship, assets that had a named beneficiary, and any property owned in a trust, passed outside the probate process to the proper owner. Next, probate assets were used to pay all valid claims against the estate. Finally, all other assets in his estate were distributed according to intestate inheritance laws of the State of Illinois in effect at the time of Lincoln's death.

State intestate laws are default rules for distribution of property when a person dies without a will. Generally, intestate property passes to the decedent's surviving spouse and closest living descendants or heirs of the person's descendants. As is well-known, Lincoln died from a gunshot wound to the head on April 15, 1865. Shortly after Lincoln's death, his son Robert sent a telegram to Supreme Court Justice David Davis asking him to handle Lincoln's estate as court-appointed administrator. The family wrote a letter to the judge of the Sangemon County Court in Illinois asking that he appoint Justice Davis administrator of Lincoln's estate, which he did.

In his initial filing with the Illinois state court, Justice Davis estimated Lincoln's estate to be worth sixty-five thousand dollars and stated it was to be divided among Mary Todd Lincoln and their two sons, Robert and Thomas, in equal shares. Mary could have requested an additional cash allowance as a widow, but she declined. Congress voted to give Mary the tax-free equivalent of one year in salary for a US president (twenty-five thousand dollars) in addition to the money from Lincoln's estate. His estate was settled in November 1867, listing a final total value of $110,296.80 (worth approximately $1.6 million in 2020 dollars). Justice Davis took no compensation for his services as administrator of the Lincoln estate.

The next famous will we examine was drafted by Queen Victoria in her own hand in 1897.

Queen Victoria.[95]

Queen Victoria drafted her last will and testament at Balmoral, her private residence in Scotland. Her last will is preserved in Windsor Castle, England. Victoria left written instructions to her staff listing personal objects she wished included in her coffin when she was buried. These items included a cast of her husband, Prince Albert's hand; one of his cloaks; photographs of Prince Albert; and one of his handkerchiefs. In addition, she listed several of her lockets and bracelets, wedding rings, a photograph of John Brown (one of her private servants), and a lock of Brown's hair wrapped in tissue. Finally, Queen Victoria asked her servants to include a sprig of Balmoral heather in her coffin and ordered that a layer of charcoal be placed under her body.

Queen Victoria specifically mentioned John Brown and Annie MacDonald (her faithful servants) in her will and commended them for their service. The Queen left 140,000 pounds each to her children Prince Albert, Princess Christian, Princess Louise, and Princess Beatrice. An English pound in 1890 would be worth around 122 pounds in 2020, so these bequests to her children would be worth around $17 million each today. The Duchess of Albany and several of her grandchildren were also given substantial bequests in Victoria's will. Queen Victoria's oldest son and successor to the throne of England, King Edward VII, inherited the bulk of her considerable fortune, including Balmoral, her country home in Scotland, and Osborne, her residence on the Isle of Wright. Queen Victoria died on January 22, 1901, at age 81. Her total estate at the time of her death was estimated by the Boston Globe at $100 million. Victoria accumulated this considerable fortune by saving part of her yearly stipend from Parliament, accumulating inheritances she received from her subjects, and the inheritance she received from her husband, Prince Albert, when he died,

Next, we review President Franklin Roosevelt's will.

Franklin D. Roosevelt.[96]

Roosevelt executed his will on November 12, 1941, approximately three weeks before Pearl Harbor was bombed by the Japanese Navy, bringing the United States into World War II. His will was witnessed by three persons. Roosevelt directed that all his just debts and funeral expenses be paid as soon after his death as practicable and that all taxes be paid out of his estate. He also requested that a simple stone be placed over his grave and the grave of his wife in the garden of his property in Hyde Park, New York. Roosevelt gave five thousand dollars to St. James Church, Hyde Park, to be used for upkeep of the Roosevelt family burial lots. Roosevelt donated the land he owned in the State of Georgia to the Georgia Warm Springs Foundation, along with all buildings and improvements on the land and all personal property in the buildings.

He gave one hundred dollars to each servant he personally employed. Roosevelt gave to his wife, Ann Eleanor Roosevelt, all his tangible personal property for use during her lifetime, except for the property in Georgia. Any items that his wife did not want were to be given to the children of his deceased children. Roosevelt stated that the children should agree unanimously about the selections, and if they were unable to do that, then his executors and his children should jointly make the determination of who received which item of Roosevelt's personal property.

Roosevelt gave his home in Hyde Park, New York, to the US government along with most of the personal property in the house. Roosevelt directed that the US government could display items from his Hyde Park home in the Franklin D. Roosevelt Library or at the home in Hyde Park as the government wished. Any personal items not accepted by his children or the US government were to be sold by his executors and the funds added to the residual of his estate. He also stated that when his wife died, his trustees should dispose of his remaining personal property as they saw fit. Roosevelt placed the remainder of his estate in trust and named his son James Roosevelt and his friend Basil T. Hackett as trustees. Roosevelt ordered that his trustees pay one-half the net income from the residuary trust to his wife in quarterly installments for the term of her natural life. The other half of the net income from his estate was to be paid to his private secretary, Marguerite A. Le Hand, in such amounts and at such times as his trustees determined in their sole discretion, not to exceed one thousand dollars annually.

Roosevelt also gave his wife, Eleanor, the use of his lands in Canada along with the improvements on the land during her lifetime. After the death of his wife, Roosevelt directed that one-half of the principal remaining in the trust be distributed to his children and the issue of his deceased children per stirpes and not per capita. The remaining half of the trust principal was to be divided into as many equal shares as there were living children and surviving grandchildren of deceased children,. The trustees were to pay the net income of these shares to the children quarterly during the term of their natural lives in a manner similar to an annuity. On the death of each child, that share shall be divided and paid to the surviving children in equal shares per stirpes and not per capita.

Roosevelt gave his executors broad powers to sell, lease, mortgage, and otherwise manage his estate and to retain property at their sole discretion, and he appointed his son James Roosevelt and his friends Basil O'Connor and Henry T. Hackett executors of his estate.

The next will we describe was drafted by President John F. Kennedy.

John F. Kennedy.[97]

Kennedy executed his last will on June 18, 1954, in Washington D.C. He revoked all prior wills and codicils and directed his executors to pay all just debts and funeral expenses as soon as convenient. He gave twenty-five thousand dollars cash to his wife Jacqueline B. Kennedy together with all his personal effects owned at the time of his death. Kennedy directed his executors to divide his remaining estate into two equal parts. He gave one share to his wife if she survived him, in trust for her benefit. He ordered his trustees to pay her stipends semiannually in such amounts as his trustees felt was appropriate.

At the death of his wife, his trustees were directed to pay over his wife's portion of the estate as stated in her will, but if she did not designate the disposition of the trust assets in her will, Kennedy directed that those assets owned in trust should be divided into as many equal parts as there were living children of them both at her death. Kennedy gave his trustees the ability to invade principal (up to 10 percent annually) as needed to support his wife. If his wife did not survive him, Kennedy directed that her share be added to the other share and distributed as directed later in his will.

Kennedy instructed that the second part of his estate be divided into as many equal shares as there were living children at the time of his death, and these funds were to be invested and reinvested to earn income, which was to be paid in annual or sooner installments, as determined by his trustees for as long as his children shall live. At the death of any child, the balance of his or her trust assets was to be paid to any living issue of the deceased child in equal shares per stirpes. If there was no issue, the deceased child's share would be paid into the trust for the benefit of the remaining surviving children. The trustees were authorized to invade the principal of the trust for the health, education, and support of his children up to a total of 20 percent of the principal of the trust.

Kennedy also stipulated that if his children did not survive him and his wife did, she should receive the second equal share of his estate. If neither his wife nor any children survived him, Kennedy stipulated that his estate should be distributed to persons, in the same proportion, as if he had died intestate. Kennedy also gave his trustees broad powers to administer the trust, including at their sole discretion the ability to distribute income from the trust at any time. He directed that all estate and other taxes should be paid by his estate.

Kennedy appointed his wife, Jacqueline B. Kennedy, and his brothers Robert F. Kennedy and Edward M. Kennedy as executors and trustees of his estate and trust. If they were unable or unwilling to serve as executors or trustees, he appointed Eunice K. Shriver, Patricia Lawford, and Jean Kennedy as successor executors and trustees. Kennedy died of a gunshot wound on November 22, 1963, in Dallas, Texas.

Next, we discuss the will of Prime Minister Winston Churchill.

Winston Churchill.[98]

Churchill executed his will on October 20, 1961, before two witnesses. Churchill added two codicils to his will at a later date. His will was probated February 9, 1965, approximately a month after his death at age ninety. Churchill appointed his wife, Clementine; his daughter Mary Soames; and John Rupert Colville as executors and trustees of his estate; they were to be paid five hundred pounds each if they agreed to administer his estate. Churchill asked to be buried in the churchyard of Bladon in Oxford County.

Churchill gave his wife all recordings of his speeches, all his articles and unfinished manuscripts, and all his other literary works with full benefit of copyright. He mentioned a deed of settlement (dated 1946) in his will and stated that he had parted with all interest therein (the deed of settlement formed a joint stock company, similar to a trust, and had trustees to administer his papers and legacy). Churchill gave all his state papers to his wife, but if she died before him, then they went to the trustees of the 1946 deed of settlement joint stock company. He also gave all his many public awards to the trustees of the 1946 deed of settlement joint stock company, to be distributed to his heirs in succession. He asked that they maintain the awards and make reproductions of them to be displayed at Chartwell, his family home.

Churchill gave all his personal property to his wife. He asked that his wife return a gold cigar case to the current Earl of Birkenhead and stated that she should feel free to sell any of the several paintings by him he had given her over the years. Churchill noted that his private home, Chartwell, had been accepted by the English National Trust, and he asked his wife to make a list of his personal items that were suitable to be displayed in the house as a proper museum. He also noted that he would leave a list with his will of personal items he wanted his wife to give to various individuals at his death.

Next, Churchill listed eight individuals who would receive various sums of money (he gave his private secretary the sum of five thousand pounds, for example). He left four thousand pounds to be distributed among his employees at his death. Churchill left to Grace Hamblin, Winston and Clementine's private secretary for many years, an annuity of five hundred pounds annually to be paid quarterly during her lifetime.

Churchill gave his son-in-law Arthur John Soames broodmares and fillies "not exceeding three in number or seven thousand pounds total." Churchill also gave his son-in-law the option to purchase all the horses, a farm, and a freehold cottage he owned at the price set by the estate duty agency. If his son-in-law chose not to exercise the option, Churchill directed that these items be sold and added to the residual of his estate. Churchill asked that his executor and trustee pay all his debts. After paying his debts, Churchill directed that the remainder of his estate be split into three equal parts, with one share going to his wife and the other two shares to any of his children living at the time of his death in equal amounts. If his wife died before him, he directed that her share be given to his living children. Churchill also stated that if any of his children died before him and left offspring, those children would take that child's share.

Churchill gave his trustees wide discretion in the investing of his funds after his death and exonerated his trustees for any potential loss of funds for any reason, including investment losses made in good faith and for the negligence or fraud of agents employed by the trustee, except willful fraud by a trustee, who then ought to be made liable for the loss.

On October 27, 1961, Churchill added a first codicil to his will, increasing the bequest to his private secretary to ten thousand pounds. Churchill later added a second codicil to his will on December 12, 1963, changing the terms of the 1946 deed of settlement dealing with his personal and public papers. Churchill's written will was entered into probate court February 9, 1965.

CHAPTER 7

Infamous Will Disputes

Even though famous people usually leave a substantial estate, there are family members who feel they have been slighted by their parent's last will and testament and decide to fight for a larger share of the estate. Even if they were given generous trust funds prior to their parents' deaths, some disgruntled family members still feel unhappy and decide to file suit for a larger share of their parent's money. The will disputes we discuss in this chapter are classic examples of the old adage "There is never enough money to make people happy." Moreover, family disputes about large sums of money often bring out the worst in people.

Estate of J. Seward Johnson.[99]

The battle over J. Seward Johnson's considerable estate was finally settled in 1986. The single legal issue was whether J. Seward was mentally competent to draft the will he signed on April 14, 1983, in which he left the bulk of his estate to his young second wife, Barbara Johnson, his former maid. Under the terms of Johnson's will, Barbara was to receive approximately $8 million as executor of the Johnson estate, plus an annual trustee's fee of $900,000 so long as she lived. Johnson's children alleged he was not competent to draft his last will and testament at the time he signed the document.

The children's attorneys presented numerous witnesses, including nurses and employees of the Johnsons, who testified that the elderly J. Seward did not understand what he was doing when he signed his last will. Attorneys for Mrs. Barbara Johnson presented other witnesses who claimed J. Seward was alert and mentally competent up until he died as age eighty-seven from prostate cancer. Before the trial verdict was announced, the parties settled their dispute.

Under the settlement, Mrs. Johnson received approximately $160 million from the estate generated by the Johnson & Johnson pharmaceutical company. Mr. Johnson's six children received $42 million to divide among themselves. An oceanographic institute founded by Mr. Johnson was awarded $20 million, and Mrs. Johnson agreed to pay $10 million in attorney's fees to the children as part of the settlement. J. Seward's son, J. Seward Johnson Jr. was awarded approximately $7 million in lieu of an executor's fee, and the IRS received approximately $80 million in taxes. The Johnson children were wealthy already, having received around $450 million in trusts and other gifts bequeathed by Mr. Johnson over the years, but they insisted on suing Barbara Johnson, claiming she had taken advantage of J. Seward's incompetence to induce him to draft a will leaving his remaining estate to her. Had the case not been settled, the parties were threatening to appeal any verdict, and the dispute could have continued for years.

Estate of H. L. Hunt.[100]

H. L. Hunt's son and grandson settled the dispute over their father and grandfather's estate by agreeing to a settlement involving hundreds of millions of dollars in trusts H. L. established for Margaret Hunt Hill and Hassie Hunt before he died. Both sides claimed victory, although the terms of the settlement are confidential. Generally, when a case is settled, neither side gets all it wanted—that is the nature of a negotiated settlement.

The dispute began shortly after Margaret Hunt Hill died in 2007. Al Hunt Jr. had signed a disclaimer that gifted his share of his mother

Margaret's trust to his three children. But after Al Hunt III asked for an accounting of the trust before Hunt Petroleum could be sold, Al Hunt Jr. disinherited his son, claiming the disclaimer he signed was not valid. After he was disinherited, Al Hunt III sued his father, sisters, aunts, and a cousin, accusing them of stealing money from the estate and conspiring to evade taxes. After numerous suits, a federal judge ordered both sides to try to settle their dispute—which they did after protracted negotiations. Although both sides claimed victory, the attorneys involved said the settlement was fair and neither side won—which seems accurate, because negotiations are based on give and take, and neither side usually gets all it wanted.

Estate of Brooke Astor.[101]

A settlement in the protracted dispute over what to do with Brooke Astor's estate ended in 2012 when a settlement was ratified by the probate court. The settlement specified how Ms. Brooke's approximately $100 million estate was to be distributed. The agreement directed that a Brooke Astor Fund for New York City Education be created and funded with $30 million. Additional millions were given to maintain Central Park, New York City playgrounds, Prospect Park, and several cultural institutions in New York City. The most noteworthy item in the settlement was the smaller sum Ms. Astor's son Anthony D. Marshall received: his portion of the estate was decreased from $31 million to $14.5 million because he had been convicted of stealing money from his mother before she had died. In addition to having his inheritance decreased, Mr. Marshall and his wife were barred from having any control over how the charitable bequests were allocated.

Ms. Astor played a major role in New York society for decades before suffering from dementia and passing away at age 105 in 2007. Mr. Marshall, Ms. Astor's son, and Mr. Morrissey Jr., the attorney who planned Ms. Astor's estate, were convicted of defrauding and stealing from her and were sentenced to three years in prison.

Estate of Fred Koch.[102]

The Koch twins David and Bill started fighting when they were boys. Their father hired an ex-soldier named Morris to chauffeur them around town and referee their frequent squabbles. Morris carried boxing gloves with him at all times to keep them from injuring each other during their numerous fights. Their father, Fred Koch, was a college boxer and fierce competitor who made a fortune in oil refining. Fred battled against communism all his life and raised his four boys, Frederick, Charles, David, and Bill, to be competitive and never quit. When the Koch brothers became adults, their father bequeathed his business to them. Charles and David managed Koch Industries and grew it into the second largest privately owned company in America.

While Charles and David were managing the family business, Bill became a collector of expensive homes and fine wines, a playboy, and a superb yachtsman who won the America's cup in 1991. While Frederick and Bill enjoyed their money, Charles and David worked hard managing Koch Industries and diversifying the company into chemicals, cattle, timber, and oil. Charles and David earned a fortune over the years they managed the family business. In contrast, Bill earned much less than Charles and David, and he was jealous.

The Koch Industries motto was "We are the biggest company you have never heard of" because Fred Koch wanted to stay out of the public spotlight and keep his company private. Fred Koch grew up in poor surroundings, and his father, a Dutch immigrant, become a successful newspaper owner. Fred was technically gifted and eventually became the co-owner of a huge oil engineering firm that was worth a fortune when he died.

The Koch brothers grew up in a wealthy family, but their father, Fred, wanted them to experience the pleasure of accomplishment, so he made them work for the money they received. Fred was demanding and stiff with his sons, but he wanted them well educated. Fred was disappointed in his oldest son Frederick, so he transferred his ambitions and attention to Charles, who was bright and energetic but more interested in drinking and chasing girls than studying. To instill some discipline in Charles, Fred sent him to Culver Military Academy, but Charles was expelled for drinking beer in his junior year. After begging forgiveness, Charles was reinstated at Culver and graduated with his class.

Fred's attention to Charles caused his youngest son, Bill, to become angry because he wanted his father's attention. Bill had such volatile emotions that his parents took him to a psychologist for a consultation. The psychologist told Bill's parents the cause of his volatile emotions was competition with Charles, and the only way to fix the problem was to send Charles away to boarding school, which the family did. Charles and David were natural companions, whereas Bill was shy and isolated and felt left out. From an early age, Bill was estranged from his family and in competition with Charles and David. After graduating from college, Charles and David took over management of Koch Industries, whereas Bill bought houses, collected wine, chased women, and raced sailing ships.

Bill finally joined the management of Koch Industries in 1974, but he always felt uncomfortable around Charles and David, who ran the company. On Christmas Day 1979, Bill caused a confrontation by asking his mother about the disposition of her estate. Charles told Bill to leave his mother out of their family arguments, so Bill attacked Charles instead, saying he was running Koch Industries like a dictator. Bill was never successful at running Koch Carbon, the part of Koch Industries he managed, at a profit. Bill pressed for more responsibility at Koch Industries even though he was not doing well with the authority he had.

At dinner after a large real estate deal had been signed, Bill said that Koch Industries has a reputation for "screwing over its partners." Bill also said he was concerned that the company was running into trouble with government regulators, and he didn't like the amount of money Charles was diverting to libertarian political causes. These political activities were beginning to draw attention to Koch Industries, and Bill complained that Charles and Bill were not living up to their father's idea of anonymity.

Most important, Bill was short of cash—all his assets were tied up in privately held Koch Industries stock, and there was no public market for his shares. If he wanted to raise money, Bill had to sell shares at a discount to the company. Koch Industries paid a 6 percent dividend, but Bill considered that too little for his substantial financial needs. To raise cash, Bill wanted to take the company public so he could sell his shares on the open market, but Charles opposed the idea because he didn't want the government regulating his business.

On July 3, 1980, Bill started a war with Charles and David by distributing a private letter to the shareholders of Koch Industries asking to take the company public and complaining about Charles's handling of the company finances. On July 9, 1980, the regular scheduled board meeting was tense as the members discussed the family dispute. Charles considered firing Bill but instead asked if he was interested in selling his stock. Bill said no. Bill and Frederick made a motion to expand the board and give them a more active role in managing the company. After Thanksgiving 1980, Bill and Frederick called a board meeting to discuss a change of management at Koch Industries. Frederick and Bill tried to collect a majority of votes to oust Charles as CEO of Koch Industries. David called Frederick and asked if he planned to fire Charles if they were successful in challenging his leadership of the company, and Frederick said yes. David then called Bill and asked if they intended to fire Charles, and Bill denied it. Because David already knew their plans to fire Charles from talking with Frederick, he called Bill a liar and said he was no longer David's brother.

The outcome of the vote to remove Charles as CEO of Koch Industries hinged on 4 percent of Koch stock held by one of J. Howard Marshall II's sons. J. Howard had bought a large block of Koch Industries stock from the boy's father, Fred, years before and felt loyal to Charles and David because of his close, personal relationship with their father. J. Howard told David he would buy the stock from his son to protect Charles. J. Howard's son stayed loyal to his father and sold the shares to him, ignoring a higher bid from Bill and Frederick. David and Charles had won the battle, but the family war was not over. After the revolt fell apart, the Koch board called a special meeting to decide the fate of Bill within Koch Industries. After lengthy discussion, the board voted to oust Bill from the company by a large majority, so David was able to abstain.

Charles wanted loyalty from the management of his company and decided he needed a divorce from his brother Bill and the dissident stockholders aligned with him. Charles engaged Morgan Stanley and Lehrman Brothers to value Koch Industries so he could buy out Bill and any other shareholder who wanted to sell. The bankers estimated Koch Industries was worth approximately $160 per share. Bill said that was too low and hired Goldman Sachs and Bain and Company to produce another valuation of the company stock. Bill also filed litigation against Koch Industries alleging mismanagement of the business. Charles and David filed a countersuit alleging defamation because of an unflattering story placed in *Fortune* magazine by Bill. Ultimately, Charles raised the offer for Koch Industries shares to $200, and Bill accepted. The buyout gave Bill over $470 million, but he still felt he had been cheated out of his fair share of the family business.

Two years later, Bill and Frederick filed another suit against Koch Industries and Charles, claiming that Charles had hidden assets during the settlement negotiations. Bill and Frederick joined their mother as a defendant in their litigation at a later date. This triggered so much stress their mother had a stroke, but Bill's lawyer subpoenaed her for a deposition anyway. Their mother died months later from ill health and stress caused by family discord. Before she died, their mother put a clause in her will demanding that Bill dismiss his suit against Charles and David or be disinherited from her estate.

Bill didn't like the clause directing him to dismiss his suit, so he challenged his mother's will in court, alleging that Charles and David had unduly influenced her to place the clause in the will. Bill lost his suit against his mother's will and was faced with a decision to dismiss his suit against Charles and David or lose his inheritance from his mother, which was considerable. Bill wanted to delay making that choice, so he hired private detectives to spy on Charles and David and dig up dirt on them to use in court if he thought he could win.

To protect themselves, Charles and David hired their own private detectives to spy on Bill and collect information to use at trial. Bill ultimately decided to go ahead with his suit against Charles and Koch Industries, which was scheduled for trial in 1998. During his suit against Charles and Koch Industries, Bill's sordid personal life came out in open court. One salacious tale involved a suit to evict a former Ford model from his apartment in Boston. It turned out that Bill was having sexual relations with two other women while having an affair with the Ford model. A few months after Bill won an eviction of the model from his Boston apartment, another of his girlfriends announced she was pregnant with Bill's child and moved into his Palm Beach mansion.

At trial, Charles's attorneys described the suit as sibling rivalry gone wild and a continuation of the family war that should have been settled years earlier. David was called to the stand by Bill's attorneys on the first day of the trial. When asked why he had abstained during the vote to oust Bill from Koch Industries, David said he cared about his twin brother and didn't want to sever family ties, so he abstained. David said that Bill had done some terrible things to the family, and David didn't want him to act that way because he loved him.

Frederick took the stand next and said he was not involved in Koch Industries because he pursued charitable activities and wasn't interested in the family businesses at all. His testimony was brief and not significant for the issues in the trial.

When Charles took the stand, he was modest and unassuming, testifying that he worked for Koch Industries when asked what was his profession rather than claiming he was CEO of the company. Charles testified that his father had taught the boys litigation was not the way to settle disputes; he said his father told him, "Never sue." Charles also described the Christmas when Bill accused his mother of not loving him. The trial was difficult for all the brothers.

Bill suffered from a cold during his testimony when he described Charles as a dictator. However, when Charles's attorney took Bill on cross-examination, he destroyed Bill's credibility by highlighting his many efforts to get money from the family, even if it meant breaking up the company and destroying his brothers. Bill testified he was conflicted about the business—on the one hand he was attached to the family business, but on the other hand he wanted the best price he could get for his shares. Bill admitted that greed won, and he had chased money over reconciliation with his family.

When the jury came back, the verdict was that Charles was guilty of misrepresentation, but it was not material, so there were no damages. The jury found that Charles had concealed some information during the settlement, but the hidden information was trivial and caused no harm. Charles and David were relieved, and Bill claimed a moral victory. Bill and Frederick refused to quit and took their appeals all the way to the US Supreme Court, which refused to hear the case. Once Bill was certain he would lose, he began trying to reach a settlement with his brothers over their father's possessions. There was a lot of money involved, but the most contentious items were their father's personal effects, especially several paintings that hung in the family home. The most difficult item to agree about was a portrait of their father, which currently hangs in Charles's office at Koch Industries.

After the brothers settled their dispute, Bill hosted a small dinner at his Palm Beach home. Charles was cordial but distant, not willing to forgive Bill for what he had done to the family. David still felt a strong affection for his younger twin brother and was willing to forgive and forget. Bill summed up his feelings by saying, "There's nothing more explosive or worse than blood and money."

Estate of Leona Helmsley.[103] When Leona Helmsley died in 2007 at the age of eighty-seven, few New Yorkers shed a tear. Her obituaries highlighted examples of how she mistreated employees, showed disdain for "the little people," and spent time in prison for tax fraud. She was labeled the queen of mean by the New York press. Although Mrs. Helmsley created generous charitable trusts in her will, the item that caught the public's attention was a $12 million trust for the care of her dog. The dog bit everyone in the household except Mrs. Helmsley and was hated by her staff. The animal was so pampered that its meals were prepared by a hotel chef and fed to the dog by maids.

The Helmsley estate, valued at over $5 billion, contained prime New York real estate, including 230 Park Avenue, the Tudor City apartment complex, the Empire State Building, the New York Helmsley Hotel, the Harley Hotel chain, the Ritz-Carlton hotels, the Helmsley Windsor, and assorted properties in Florida. Mrs. Helmsley was a successful New York real estate broker when she met her future husband Harry Helmsley, who fell in love with her and left his wife in 1972. The couple lived a luxurious lifestyle and owned a penthouse overlooking Central Park, a mansion in Connecticut, a home in Palm Beach, and another atop a mountain in Arizona.

Even with all her money, Mrs. Helmsley delayed paying merchants or contractors and refused to pay New York taxes. She was sued by a contractor to collect for renovation of their Connecticut home, and even after she was forced to pay, she insisted that the invoices be charged to Helmsley Hotels so she could get a tax deduction for the work. The contractor was so angry that he sent the invoices to a New York reporter, who exposed how Mrs. Helmsley did business and evaded taxes. It didn't take long for the Manhattan district attorney to indict Mr. and Mrs. Helmsley for tax fraud. At trial, a maid testified that Mrs. Helmsley said, "Only little people pay taxes." The couple was charged with evading over $1.2 million in taxes and filing false returns. Mr. Helmsley was found mentally incompetent, so Mrs. Helmsley took the blame and was sentenced to prison for tax evasion. She served eighteen months before being released.

When Harry Helmsley died in 1997, his last will and testament gave the residual of his estate to his wife. Mrs. Helmsley signed her own will in 2005 and died on August 20, 2007. She was survived by four grandchildren and her brother, although they were not the principal beneficiaries of her estate. Approximately 99 percent of her real estate empire went to the Leona M. and Harry B. Helmsley Charitable Trust, which would do beneficial work in New York City after Mrs. Helmsley's death. Her grandson Craig Panzirer and her granddaughter, Meegan Panzirer, were given nothing, and her other grandchildren, David and Walter, each received $5 million. Her brother Alvin received $5 million in cash and a trust that paid 5 percent annually to him. Mrs. Helmsley established a $3 million trust to maintain the Helmsley Mausoleum.

Given that her will disinherited two grandchildren, left $12 million in trust to care for her dog, and did not clearly identify the purpose of the charitable trust she established, it was almost certain there would be extensive litigation over her will. However, rather than spend years fighting in court, the parties wisely decided to settle their dispute. The agreement was approved by the probate court on April 20, 2008. The two disinherited grandchildren received $6 million to divide between them in the settlement, and other bequests were reduced a proportionate amount. The court also ordered the $12 million trust to care for Mrs. Helmsley's dog reduced to $2 million and transferred the balance of the $12 million to the charitable trust.

Trustees of the charitable trust asked the court for directions about how to distribute funds in the trust. The court said the trustees could apply trust funds for such charitable purposes and in such amounts as they may determine—significant discretion indeed. The trustees soon granted $36 million for health and medical research on humans and $1 million for medical research on dogs. In 2009, the trustees gave $136 million to hospitals, medical foundations, and homeless programs, as well as $1 million to various organizations caring for dogs, including the Humane Society.

Estate of J. Howard Marshall II.[104]

J. Howard Marshall II made a fortune investing in Koch Industries and married a much younger woman, Anna Nichole Smith, late in life. The combination of vast wealth, a much younger wife, and stepchildren created years of litigation, two appeals to the US Supreme Court, and millions of dollars in attorney's fees as the family fought over J. Howard's estate. After protracted litigation, the Court of Appeals for the First District in Houston threw out $500,000 in sanctions that a probate judge had ordered Anna Nichole Smith to pay her son-in-law, E. Pierce Marshall, for filing a frivolous challenge to the will of J. Howard Marshall II.

The chief justice of the appellate court also changed several parts of the earlier probate ruling. The dispute over J. Howard's estate even created a constitutional precedent when Chief Justice John Roberts wrote a ruling in *Stern v. Marshall*[105] stating that a federal statute granting bankruptcy courts the authority to decide remotely connected claims based on state law was unconstitutional. The Texas Appeals Court also decided that Anna Nichole Smith was not a beneficiary of J. Howard Marshall II's estate, confirming the earlier jury finding reached after a trial in 2001 involving hundreds of documents and days of testimony.

The case began shortly after J. Howard Marshall II died on August 4, 1995, at age ninety. After J. Howard's death, Anna Nichole Smith contested his will, which placed his Koch Industries stock in a trust for E. Pierce Marshall's benefit. Anna Nichole filed for bankruptcy in 1996, and Pierce filed a claim for defamation against her, saying that Anna Nichole lied about him scheming to take her inheritance. The bankruptcy court rejected Pierce's claim and awarded Anna Nichole Smith $475 million from the Marshall estate. In 2001, a Texas probate court ordered Anna Nichole to pay $741,000 in attorney's fees to Pierce, who then filed in federal court in California to dismiss Anna Nichole's claims, stating that they were inconsistent with jury findings in the Texas case. The federal court in California awarded Anna Nichole $44 million in sanctions due to Pierce's attorney's "egregious" behavior.

The Ninth Circuit Court of Appeals reversed the California federal court ruling, stating that the bankruptcy court had no jurisdiction because the Texas probate court had exclusive jurisdiction. Next, the US Supreme Court ruled that the statute giving a bankruptcy court jurisdiction over remotely related state court matters was unconstitutional. The federal district judge in California, upset with the tactics used by Pierce, hinted he was leaning toward ordering the Pierce estate to pay $40 million for bad faith behavior during the prior litigation. However, after studying the issue, the court ruled there was insufficient evidence to support an award of sanctions against Pierce's estate. After twenty years of litigation, the estate of J. Howard Marshall II was finally closed.

Estate of B. B. King.[106]

Several women claimed B. B. King fathered their children over the years, and he never denied their claims, although he had a low sperm count and the claims were probably not true. When he died in 2015, B. B. King left a legal mess, pitting his children against each other and his administrator, LaVerne Toney, in a protracted series of court fights. King left two conflicting trusts that triggered litigation between the children and his estate administrator.

The eleven children who survived B. B. King sued his estate administrator over two trusts signed in 2007 and 2014. The earlier trust granted generous allowances to several of King's children, whereas the 2014 trust didn't include grants to any of the children and appointed LaVerne Toney administrator of King's estate. Toney claims the 2014 trust was valid and that was the one she was following.

Because King wrote only a few of his songs and worked when black singers were not well paid, his estate was estimated to be worth only about $7 million according to *Billboard* magazine. King loved his families and paid for their support while he lived, but that comfortable system fell apart when King died. The children claimed they had not received a dime since their father had died, and they wanted to get what was owed them. The children filed suit claiming King's estate administrator had poisoned him. Ever through there was no existing evidence to support the claim, an autopsy of B. B. King's body was ordered, and the resulting examination found nothing to justify the allegation that King was murdered. Toney sued the children for defamation after the Las Vegas police released their findings. These allegations split the families, with some trying to bring peace and others filing suits against Toney for their "fair" share of the King estate.

King was handsome and liked women. The result was countless women who claimed he was the father of their child. If a woman said her child was fathered by King, he never denied it. B. B. King was busy with his music, but he found time to see his children. As King aged and his health declined, his generosity slowed. He was diabetic and suffered from high blood pressure near the end of his life. King gave Toney power of attorney to manage his business affairs after he died and appointed her trustee of his estate to protect his musical legacy. However, it wasn't clear how he wanted his assets distributed because he left two different trusts.

A few of King's children sued Toney a second time, alleging she had been taking money from King's estate for her own benefit. The suit also claimed she had neglected King's medical care during his declining years. These claims resulted in another investigation by the Las Vegas Police Department, which found no evidence for any of these later claims. Toney's attorneys produced a birth certificate showing that Karen Williams, who led the children who filed the second suit against Toney for defrauding King's estate, was not even biologically related to King. King's personal physician and dentist filed affidavits with the court stating he was always well cared for by Toney while he lived. Toney admitted there had been a theft of property from the King estate, but she said King asked her not to file a police report because he believed members of his own family were likely responsible for the theft.

The King families also asked for an accounting of the estate and claimed that the later trust was drafted while King was incompetent. The King children split into factions fighting Toney over the estate. Toney testified that she was simply trying to carry out the terms of King's last wishes, but the children disagreed with her interpretation of the trusts. The family claimed the 2014 will and trust, which were the documents Toney was following, were flawed because they were drafted when King was blind and suffering from cognitive decline. The children wanted the earlier 2007 will and trust upheld because they claimed their father was competent at the time these documents were drafted.

The probate court reviewed the 2007 and 2014 wills and trusts and confirmed Laverne Toney's control of B. B. King's estate.

The King saga is a cautionary tale. Perhaps if there were not so many children from so many different mothers, they could get along. But under current conditions, that hasn't happened. Moreover, as the King saga gained press coverage, more women started coming forward claiming King was the father of their children. Just before he died, King said to ignore any of these claims because he "wasn't taking no more kids on."

Sumner Redstone Estate.[107]

After more than two years of litigation and several contentious suits, Sumner Redstone's former girlfriend Manuela Herzer and the Redstone family finally reached a settlement of their conflicting claims to the Redstone estate. In the agreement, Herzer agreed to pay the Redstone family $3.25 million as reimbursement for gifts she received from Sumner Redstone over the years. The settlement was reached shortly before trial and was a significant loss for Herzer, who had earlier rejected a $30 million settlement offer from the Redstone family. Herzer was evicted from Sumner's mansion and disinherited in 2015. In an attempt to regain control of Redstone's estate, Herzer filed suit, making public his failing health and salacious details about his dating habits and emotional behavior.

Shari Redstone, Sumner's estranged daughter, assumed control of her father's personal and business affairs after she discovered her father was not competent to manage his businesses or himself. Herzer claimed Shari was improperly taking control of the family businesses and demanded that Redstone be examined by independent physicians. The medical experts' findings resulted in Redstone being removed from managing his businesses because of incompetence. Redstone's diagnosis triggered shareholder suits and boardroom fights over his companies. In 2016, Shari Redstone gained control of Viacom, and CBS promptly sued the Redstone family, seeking to gain voting control of their Viacom shares. That suit was dismissed after the CBS CEO was accused of sexual harassment and lost his job.

In 2016, Shari Redstone sued two of her father's former girlfriends, claiming elder abuse. She alleged his former girlfriends had conspired to isolate Sumner from his family and steal money from his companies. The suit stated that Redstone had given more than $150 million to the former girlfriends under duress and was not competent to make these gifts. *Forbes* magazine estimated that Redstone was worth more than $4.5 billion and held controlling interests in CBS and Viacom. The outcome of this saga was that Sumner's former girlfriends ended up with debts rather than a fortune. Perhaps there's a lesson in that outcome: greed doesn't pay.

CHAPTER 8

Notorious Business Trusts

During the nineteenth and twentieth centuries, aggressive business owners began using business trusts to consolidate related companies into a single enterprise with the power to set prices and limit the supply of commodities offered to the market. These monopoly business trusts were first developed in the United States during the American Civil War to limit competition and gain economies and efficiencies of scale for the business trust managers.

Where did these business trusts originate and how did they work?

Origin of Business Trusts

The idea of using a trust to consolidate and manage related businesses was developed by Samuel C. T. Dodd, Standard Oil's general counsel, during the American Civil War so John D. Rockefeller could consolidate control over the refining and distribution of kerosene.[108] Dodd developed the business trust to centralize control of an entire industry, bringing order and economies of scale to the oil business and reducing competition. The business trust allowed companies that joined Standard Oil trust to cooperate and hold the price of kerosene constant, claiming this benefited American consumers. Economists at the time believed business trust monopolies would reduce ruinous competition and bring order, stability, and reasonable prices to American consumers. After careful study, however, the US government discovered that business trusts were using unfair monopoly tactics to reduce competition and earn huge profits for themselves at the expense of consumers by manipulating the supply of commodities offered to market to maintain high prices.

Ultimately, criticisms of business trusts by journalists, the public, and Congress led to passage of the Sherman Antitrust Act, a federal statute designed to encourage competition within industries and limit the formation of monopoly trusts. Business trusts were investigated, charged, tried, convicted of restraint of trade, and forced to break up through application of the Sherman Antitrust Act by the U.S. Justice Department and the U.S. Supreme Court. Business trusts were gradually phased out in favor of holding companies, which are limited in their power to restrain trade and exercise monopoly pricing power.

What is the Sherman Antitrust Act, and what does it do?

The Sherman Antitrust Act

The Sherman Antitrust Act was passed by Congress in 1890 to limit anticompetitive agreements and monopoly market activities among American businesses.[109] The US Justice Department was authorized by the act to investigate and sue any entity, company, or group that limits competition. The Sherman Act, as it was eventually named, was intended to keep businesses from artificially restricting the supply of goods coming to market so they could control the prices they charged consumers. The act prohibits illegal agreements among businesses designed to reduce competition and artificially raise prices above fair market values. Its purpose is to maintain a competitive market place in America. The act, designed to encourage competition among American businesses, was passed by Congress during the Benjamin Harrison administration. The Sherman Act prohibits anticompetitive agreements and monopoly market arrangements among American businesses. The act authorizes the US Justice

Department to investigate and bring suit against any association that limits competition. It also gives private citizens the right to sue for triple damages against a business that is convicted of antitrust violations.

The purpose of the Sherman Antitrust Act is to prohibit price manipulation through restricted competition in a market. A monopoly that develops because one business is more efficient than its competition is not affected by the Sherman Act—it doesn't protect businesses from effective competition. The Sherman Act is designed to prevent illegal secret agreements among businesses to create a monopoly and raise prices artificially by restricting the supply of goods coming to market. The Sherman Act protects consumers by maintaining a competitive marketplace.

The Sherman Act was passed in response to monopolistic business trusts that controlled the supply of good offered to consumers, suppressed competition, and artificially raised prices. The act's goal was to prevent the restriction of free competition among American businesses by trust agreements that limited the supply of commodities coming to market, artificially raised prices, and defrauded consumers. The act outlawed any business activity or association that restrained trade. The Sherman Act is divided into three parts: Section 1 prohibits specific types of anticompetitive actions, Section 2 deals with results that are anticompetitive, and Section 3 extends the jurisdiction of the Sherman Act to US territories and the District of Columbia.

Congress passed a second antitrust act in 1914 to deal with newer anticompetitive practices developed by businesses in response to the Sherman Antitrust Act.

The Clayton Antitrust Act.[110]

The Clayton Antitrust Act prohibits additional activities deemed anticompetitive by Congress, including price discrimination intended to create a monopoly, exclusive sales agreements, arrangements that tied products together (called bundling) so the consumer couldn't buy one item without the other, and mergers or acquisitions that tended to reduce competition among certain businesses.

The US Justice Department began applying the Sherman Act and then the Clayton Antitrust Act to monopoly business practices almost immediately after they were passed by Congress. During the twentieth century, over half a dozen monopolies were dissolved through Supreme Court decisions or out-of-court settlements with the US Justice Department. Business trusts are still used today, but only to manage company pension plans, stock mutual funds, family businesses, and employee tax withholding plans.

The first and perhaps best-known business trust was organized by John D. Rockefeller in 1863 and was called the Standard Oil Trust.

The Standard Oil Trust

The Standard Oil Trust was established by John D. Rockefeller to consolidate the oil industry in America.[111] By 1868, Standard Oil was the largest refiner in the world, producing primarily kerosene for home lighting. Rockefeller consolidated his oil businesses into a single monopoly trust and then invited other owners of oil businesses to transfer their shares to the Standard Oil Trust in return for an interest in profits from the trust. Standard Oil Trust ultimately owned fourteen oil corporations and exercised control over twenty-six others, creating a monopoly in the production, refining, transportation, and marketing of kerosene in America. A board of trustees managed the affairs of Standard Oil Trust. Rockefeller himself owned 41 percent of the trust certificates and effectively controlled board decisions. Rockefeller claimed he established Standard Oil Trust to improve the organization and efficiency of his many business interests, but he was soon accused of abusing his market power by artificially holding prices for kerosene at a steady, high level and limiting competition.

The Standard Oil Trust organized committees to control crude oil exploration, production, refining, transportation, and marketing, stabilizing the price Americans paid for kerosene to light their homes. However, the stable price of kerosene didn't necessarily represent a benefit to consumers because the price of discovering, drilling, and pumping crude oil; transporting and refining the oil into kerosene; and distributing the kerosene to consumers decreased substantially under the direction and control of the Standard Oil Trust. Large new oil fields were discovered, pipelines were installed to move crude oil to refineries, and improvements in the efficiencies of oil refining plants and distribution systems lowered the cost of discovering, producing, refining, moving, and marketing kerosene. Rather than pass these savings on to customers, Rockefeller and his trust partners pocketed the excess profits and held the price of kerosene steady for years by managing the supply offered for sale. Customers didn't complain because they were able to buy plentiful amounts of kerosene at a stable price, and they were unaware of the huge profits Standard Oil was making.

Before the invention of the internal combustion engine for motor vehicles, gasoline was a worthless by-product of refining kerosene and was of little interest to Rockefeller. After the invention of the automobile, however, gasoline became Standard Oil's most important product and earned the trust hundreds of millions in profits. By joining several oil businesses into a single monopoly trust, Rockefeller gained control over the price consumers paid for kerosene and gasoline, limited competition, and collected huge profits. Other businessmen saw the advantages of using a business trust to consolidate ownership of companies in an industry so they developed monopolies in steel, tobacco, ship transportation, diamonds and matches.

The Standard Oil Trust was broken up through antitrust litigation in 1911. However, many of the smaller oil companies formed after the breakup of the Standard Oil Trust kept the name Standard Oil, continued in the petroleum business, and still dominated the industry, becoming more valuable than the old Standard Oil Trust through the refining and sale of gasoline.

The next business trust we examine is US Steel, organized and controlled by Wall Street banker J. P. Morgan.

The US Steel Trust

J. P. Morgan founded US Steel in 1901 as the first billion-dollar corporation.[112] He formed a business trust that controlled 60 percent of the steel industry and employed nearly 170,000 workers. What was a New York banker doing running a steel company? The story began in the 1890s when Morgan shifted from financing railroads to buying and consolidating steel companies into a single massive business trust. Andrew Carnegie, owner of the largest steel company in America at the time, was not impressed—he predicted that Morgan, a New York banker who knew little about running a giant steel company, would fail trying to manage a steel business. Morgan wanted Carnegie to join him and form a steel trust that would limit competition in America, be more efficient, and enjoy huge profits by controlling the supply of steel that came to market. Carnegie was not interested because he liked competition.

Morgan got the idea to form US Steel while listening to a speech on December 12, 1900, delivered by Charles Schwab, Carnegie's chief assistant, describing the possibility of a vertically integrated business trust that would own companies making everything from raw steel to finished steel tubes. Morgan was so impressed with the idea that he called Schwab and asked him to meet at Morgan's home on Madison Avenue. Morgan met Schwab several times and then offered to buy Carnegie's steel company because he would not join Morgan in forming a steel trust. Carnegie thought about the proposal overnight and gave Schwab a slip of paper with $480 million written on it. When Morgan saw the price, he accepted the deal.

Morgan's next goal was to buy the iron ore holdings owned by Rockefeller in the Mesabi Range of Minnesota. Morgan hated Rockefeller and vowed he would never meet him personally. However, Morgan eventually decided he needed the iron ore, so he agreed to meet Rockefeller at his home on West Fifty-Fourth Street in New York. When they were seated in the same room, Rockefeller told Morgan he was retired and would not discuss a business proposition at his home. Instead, Rockefeller told Morgan, "This meeting is just a social call," and Morgan could discuss buying his iron ore deposits with Rockefeller's son at a later date. John D. Rockefeller Jr. came to Morgan's offices a few days later to negotiate a sale of the iron ore. They agreed on a price of $88.5 million for the iron ore and ships used to transport ore to the steel mills. After acquiring the iron ore and ships from Rockefeller, Morgan owned or controlled a majority of America's steel industry and monopolized the business for decades before the US Department of Justice sued US Steel for monopolistic practices and unlawful restraint of trade. US Steel was then separated into several smaller steel manufacturing companies.

The next business trust we discuss is the American Tobacco Company.

The American Tobacco Company

The American Tobacco Company had its origins in a tobacco business managed by James B. Duke.[113] American Tobacco Company eventually dominated the US tobacco market during the first half of the twentieth century. The company started when James Duke joined his father, Washington Duke, in manufacturing cigarettes in Durham, North Carolina. Advances in cigarette manufacturing techniques allowed the rapid expansion of cigarette production in America, and Duke took advantage of the volume of cigarettes he was able to produce with improved manufacturing machines to integrate the tobacco industry from top to bottom and expand his markets by aggressive business practices.

Duke grew his cigarette business by lowering prices and spending heavily on advertising. However, intense competition from other cigarette manufacturing firms limited his profits, so Duke began searching for a better business model to make more money. After New Jersey passed a statute allowing a holding company to own several related businesses, Duke convinced his competitors to merge into a single entity called the American Tobacco Company, which ultimately controlled almost 90 percent of the US market for cigarettes. Duke negotiated an agreement between his company and Allen and Gintner, Kinney Tobacco Co., William S. Kimball and Co., and Goodwin and Co., to form American Tobacco, which monopolized the cigarette industry. Duke then negotiated a contract with the company that manufactured cigarette making machines and vertically integrated his tobacco business, combining enterprises that specialized in buying tobacco leaves, manufacturing cigarettes, and selling the finished produce in Duke's own retail tobacco stores. Duke eliminated less profitable cigarette brands and concentrated his advertising on a few popular and profitable ones.

Duke continued to buy smaller tobacco companies and eventually controlled most of the chewing tobacco and snuff market in America in addition to cigarette sales. The American Tobacco Company became so powerful that it was eventually ordered to break into smaller companies by the US Supreme Court. The US Justice Department filed suit against the American Tobacco Company in 1907 and by 1911 had won an antitrust judgment under the Sherman Act, convicting the American Tobacco Company of "unreasonable business practices," including monopoly practices and restraint of trade.

Even after being broken up by the US Supreme Court, the American Tobacco Company controlled a significant portion of the US cigarette market because it was allowed to keep successful brands such as Pall Mall cigarettes, which the company aggressively marketed. However, over the next several decades, the American Tobacco Company began to lose market share to R. J. Reynolds, which heavily advertised Camel cigarettes and eventually controlled over a third of the cigarette market in America. The US Justice Department broke up the American Tobacco Company, increased competition among tobacco manufacturers, and lowered the price of cigarettes, increasing the number of Americans who were killed by smoking—an unfortunate unintended consequence.

Next, we review De Beers Corporation, which developed a monopoly in mining and marketing diamonds.

The De Beers Diamond Trust

By 1990, the De Beers diamond cartel controlled the marketing of over 90 percent of the world's diamonds.[114] However, market factors and antitrust litigation eventually caused this famous monopoly to lose its marketing dominance. Competitors began selling diamonds outside the De Beers marketing cartel, and the US Justice Department filed suit against De Beers for unfair restraint of trade and forced it to change its monopoly marketing practices.

The company was named after a huge diamond mine discovered on the De Beers farm in South Africa. Cecil Rhodes founded his monopoly diamond marketing trust by buying the mining claim on De Beers' farm. The company eventually became De Beers Consolidated Mines, Ltd. By accumulating other mining claims in the area, Rhodes was able to manipulate the supply of diamonds offered for sale and expand the market for diamonds by aggressively focusing on distribution, advertising, and sale of diamonds worldwide. Rhodes developed an efficient distribution and marketing system and convinced other diamond mining companies to market their production through his company. promising that De Beers would control the supply and therefore the price of diamonds, guaranteeing cooperating companies a handsome profit if they joined his marketing cartel. De Beers controlled the price of diamonds by manipulating the supply of cut diamonds offered for sale in the world market.

In 1914, De Beers Consolidated Mines, Ltd., sent Ernest Oppenheimer to South Africa to survey its mining claims. Oppenheimer reported that the De Beers claims were in an alluvial field where diamonds were found close to or on the surface and could be mined efficiently without digging deep into the earth. While in South Africa, Oppenheimer saw an opportunity for himself and bought German mining claims during the early months of World War I. The Germans were willing to sell at a reasonable price because they believed the British would confiscate their holdings in South Africa during the war. Once Oppenheimer controlled a significant share of the existing diamond mining claims in South Africa, he sent an ultimatum to De Beers stating that if the company didn't make him chairman of De Beers Consolidated Mines, Ltd., Oppenheimer would flood the market with diamonds and drive De Beers out of business. The company agreed, and he became chairman of De Beers in 1929. The De Beers cartel limited the supply of diamonds offered for sale during the Great Depression and survived those difficult financial times in good order.

During World War II, the United States wanted to buy industrial diamonds from De Beers for use in precision manufacturing, but the company refused to sell America any diamonds, fearing that after the war was over, surplus diamonds would be dumped on the market and the price would fall. Eventually, the United States and De Beers reached a compromise allowing the diamond monopoly to maintain an office in Canada so De Beers could keep the supply of diamonds out of US control and still sell diamonds to American industry. There were rumors that Germany was smuggling diamonds out of the Congo, but that was never verified.

To control prices and keep them high, Oppenheimer and De Beers manipulated the supply of diamonds offered for sale. In a weak market, such as during the Great Depression, De Beers reduced the supply of diamonds available for sale. When market demand for diamonds became strong after the Second World War, the company released more gems for sale. Oppenheimer and De Beers were able to control diamond marketing until late in the twentieth century, when economic competition and suits in the United States under the Sherman Act destroyed the De Beers diamond monopoly.

By the 1980s, De Beers was selling diamonds worth nearly two billion dollars in America alone. However, several things happened that broke De Beers' monopoly control of the diamond trade. First, the Soviet Union disintegrated, and Russia began selling diamonds outside the De Beers marketing and distribution system to make a quick profit because the government needed money. At the same time, the US Justice Department filed an antitrust suit against De Beers. Then Rio Tinto, a huge mining company, broke with De Beers and began selling diamonds through Argyle Diamonds instead. Finally, a class-action civil suit charging price fixing was filed in US federal court against the De Beers corporation by a group of American plaintiffs.

De Beers settled the Sherman Antitrust case against it in the United States and a similar antitrust case in Europe. The company also settled all civil class action suits against it for conspiring to fix the price of diamonds, sponsoring false and misleading advertising, and unlawfully monopolizing the diamond supply. De Beers paid approximately $300 million to the class action plaintiffs and their attorneys and agreed to stop violating federal and state antitrust statutes. Because of these legal problems, De Beers share of the diamond trade dropped below 35 percent.

Eventually, De Beers mines in South Africa were depleted, and the company began manufacturing and selling diamonds under the Lightbox label. The company began a new business strategy focusing on its own brand of manufactured diamonds rather than trying to convince others to join the De Beers marketing company. While it enjoyed monopoly control of diamond sales, the Oppenheimer family accumulated one of the largest fortunes in the world.

We turn next to the International Mercantile Marine Co., a business trust formed early in the twentieth century by J. P. Morgan to monopolize passenger travel on transatlantic routes.

International Mercantile Marine Co

This shipping cartel combined the American Line, Red Star Line, Atlantic Transport Line, White Star Line, the Leyland Line, and the Dominion Line into a single business entity controlled by J. P. Morgan.[115] After merging several shipping companies into the International Mercantile Marine Co. (IMM), Morgan negotiated a profit-sharing agreement with German Hamburg-Amerika and the North German Lloyd shipping lines to expand his control of transatlantic passenger travel. Morgan's goal was to dominate transatlantic shipping, but he failed because of American antitrust litigation, opposition from the British government, competition from British shipping companies, and travelers' preference for flying across the Atlantic rather than slowly sailing across the ocean.

In spite of Morgan's backing, the International Mercantile Marine Co. suffered cash flow problems and defaulted on interest payments in 1914, partly as a result of bad publicity and financial problems associated with the sinking of RMS *Titanic*. The cartel went through receivership, reorganized its finances, and emerged as a stronger company in 1916 when the shipping business was revived by demand for moving troops and supplies to Europe during World War I.

In its early years, the International Mercantile Marine Co. prospered, helped by steady immigration from Europe to the United States. The company carried nearly sixty-five thousand passengers across the Atlantic in 1902. However, competition from British Cunard Line proved costly for IMM. The Cunard Line was subsidized by the British government to build two giant new ocean liners that Britain could use to move troops and materials during a war. These two giant ships, the *Lusitania* and *Mauretania*, were placed in service in 1907, and competition from these super-liners forced IMM to build three large ocean liners of its own—RMS *Olympic*, RMS *Titanic*, and HMHS *Britannic*—at enormous expense.

The sinking of IMM's ocean liner *Titanic* on April 15, 1912, on her first voyage across the Atlantic caused serious financial and reputational damage to the company. Aside from the enormous loss of human life during the sinking of the *Titanic* (over 1,500 died), IMM also lost an expensive ocean liner, as well as its reputation for safety and reliability. The loss of the *Titanic* also brought increased regulatory scrutiny to IMM. The American commission of inquiry investigating causes of the *Titanic* shipwreck highlighted the monopoly nature of IMM, and the company was criticized by members of the US Senate for its anticompetitive business practices.

IMM eventually failed for financial reasons rather than because of antitrust litigation. It went into bankruptcy in 1986 because airplanes became the preferred way for passengers to travel across the Atlantic.

Our final business trust was formed by Ivar Kreuger, the Match King. He eventually developed his business trust into a gigantic Ponzi scheme that defrauded thousands of investors of millions in the 1930s.

The Match King

Ivar Kreuger was hailed as the savior of Europe after World War I because his company made low-interest loans to bankrupt countries. Swedish Match was one of the most respected companies in the world during the 1920s, and because Kreuger's businesses had a better credit rating that many European governments, he was able to offer loans to financially distressed countries at a lower interest rate than they could attract in the open financial marketplace.[116] Kreuger made a profit by taking out low-interest loans based on his company's good credit and reselling these loans to financially distressed governments at a higher interest rate that was still lower than the governments could attract on the open market. Kreuger wanted to expand his financial business, so he began to use shares of Swedish Match to buy other companies. Eventually, Kreuger overextended and transformed his business trust into a huge Ponzi scheme that defrauded thousands of investors when it failed a few years after the 1929 stock market crash in America.

Kreuger was born in 1880 in Sweden and emigrated to the United States when he was twenty years old. For several years, he worked on construction projects around the world and became an expert on reinforced concrete construction. He returned to Sweden in 1907, formed a business partnership with a young Swedish engineer named Toll, and went into the construction business. Kreuger expanded his business into Finland, Russia, and Germany and formed Swedish Match in 1917. Kreuger the builder and Krueger the match maker ran legitimate businesses during these early years and made money constructing buildings, selling matches, and making loans to financially strapped governments. By 1923, Kreuger and Toll was extraordinarily successful, but that wasn't enough for Ivar Kreuger. He wanted to expand further, so he shifted his focus from manufacturing and construction to growing his loan-making business and began paying high dividends to attract capital and increase the price of his company stock.

Kreuger built match factories around the world and bought several other companies, including Ericsson Telephone, which still exists today. He also owned the Swedish Film Industry Company and a pulp business. After 1923, Kreuger began to artificially manipulate the price of his stock so he could buy other businesses by paying higher and higher dividends out of capital, eventually developing a classic Ponzi scheme. Every Ponzi scheme is doomed to fail sooner or later because the cost of paying high dividends exceeds the company's income, so the owner is eventually forced to pay his stockholders out of capital, guaranteeing he will eventually go broke. Krueger's empire began to crumble in October 1929 after the New York Stock Market crashed.

Krueger tried several desperate measures to restore confidence in his business, including a loan of $125 million to the German government that he couldn't afford and the forging of nearly 29 million pounds in Italian government bonds. He listed most of the fake Italian bonds on Kreuger and Toll's balance sheet to make his company appear solvent. This financial sleight of hand worked for a few months until the next set of dividend payments came due. Kreuger had no choice but to sell Ericsson Telephone to raise cash and pay the dividend if he wanted to keep his Ponzi scheme afloat. Kreuger arranged an exchange of stock between IT&T and Ericsson along with a payment of $11 million to Kreuger.

Kreuger had postponed disaster for a few months, but the end was near. IT&T auditors began looking at Ericsson's books in detail and discovered a 27 million kroner asset that was nothing but a claim by Ericsson on Kreuger's other businesses—in other words, worthless paper because there was no collateral attached to the loan. With his empire collapsing, Kreuger became more distracted and despondent. Eventually his business empire failed, and Kreuger was tried, convicted, and sent to prison for financial fraud. No one is certain how much money disappeared in Kreuger's Ponzi scheme; estimates range from $250 million to over $400 million. His US operations were declared bankrupt in August 1932, and US stockholders recovered about thirty cents of every dollar they invested in his Ponzi scheme.

To avoid a repeat of Kreuger's Ponzi scheme, Congress established the Securities Exchange Commission (SEC) to regulate stock market activities, prosecute stock market fraud, and monitor insider trading in securities. A few years later, Congress passed the Trust Indenture Act to regulate the type and amount of collateral required to make a loan in the United States in an effort to avoid another Ponzi scheme similar to the one Kreuger ran.

Prosecution of Business Trusts

The US Justice Department filed antitrust cases against business associations suspected of restraining trade shortly after the Sherman Act was passed in 1890. As a result of these antitrust investigations, the Chesapeake and Ohio Fuel Company trust was dissolved in 1902, Northern Securities Trust was disbanded in 1904, Standard Oil Trust was broken up in 1906, and in 1911 the American Tobacco Co. was divided into four new entities. Later, General Electric Co., Philips, Sylvania, Tungsol, Consolidated Chicago Miniature, Corning, and Westinghouse agreed to sign consent decrees admitting they had violated the Sherman Antitrust Act. However, the Federal Baseball Club, which managed America's pastime, was exempted from the Sherman Act because it was judged to not engage in interstate commerce and was not covered by the act. In 1982, AT&T Company agreed to a breakup through negotiations with the US Justice Department, and Microsoft Corporation settled with the US Justice Department in 2001 without the company being broken up. Microsoft was required to modify its business practices to allow more competition in the computer industry.

Some believe the Sherman Act is a mixed blessing for business and consumers, however.

Criticisms of the Sherman Antitrust Act

Economists and judges have criticized the Sherman Act on grounds of market efficiency. For example, economist Alan Greenspan has argued that the Sherman Act stifles innovation and harms American consumers by causing capital to be allocated in nonoptimal ways through the judicial process rather than the market place. Judges Robert Bork and Richard Posner have proposed that the Sherman Act should be evaluated for economic efficiency as well as restraint of trade. They argued that inefficient cartels would be eliminated by market forces alone, and there would be no need for the Sherman Antitrust Act in most cases.

CONCLUSIONS

The laws of inheritance have become more democratic over the years because of pressures from legislatures, lawyers, citizens, and courts. Laws governing wills and trusts often appear rigid and arbitrary to the average executor or beneficiary, and the probating of a will may seem bureaucratic and complicated, but the courts and lawyers insist these procedures are necessary to ensure the terms of a will are followed properly. American inheritance laws borrowed heavily from English common law during the colonial period and then evolved in their own way after the American Revolution. Modern legislatures, lawyers, and courts are trying to simplify the laws of succession and make them easier to use and understand.

Uniform International Wills Act

Many countries, including the United States, have adopted the Uniform International Wills Act, making a will drafted in any signatory country valid in any other country that has signed the act.[117] The Uniform International Wills Act allows an individual to move to any signatory country without having to draft a new will. American inheritance laws are becoming more flexible, and probate procedures are becoming simpler. For example, a self-proving affidavit is now available in most states so an executor doesn't have to bring a live witness into probate court to prove a will was properly executed. Also, a copy of the will can be filed and proved in court by witnesses if the original is lost.

There are now alternate ways to pass assets to the next generation.

Alternatives to a Will

Drafting a will is no longer the only way to organize an estate and pass assets to the next generation. Many individuals are using living trusts to hold assets during their lifetime and pass them on to beneficiaries at death without having to go through probate. Moreover, the Totten Trust (a bank or brokerage account in which the settlor places money with instructions that any funds remaining in the account be paid to a named beneficiary on the death of the settlor) is available to anyone who has a bank or brokerage account and wants to leave money in the account to a named beneficiary who survives the account holder.[118] These accounts are also called pay on death (POD) accounts and are easy to establish at a bank or brokerage house.

American laws of succession have changed over the years to meet evolving needs of ordinary citizens rather than the rich and powerful. Because families are smaller and people are living longer, government programs such as Social Security, Medicare, and the estate tax have changed modern estate planning. Since the introduction of Social Security and Medicare, older Americans feel less need to save for retirement or buy life insurance to safeguard the welfare of widows and children when a wage earner dies. Older Americans are not relying so heavily on their families for economic support, staying independent longer, and retiring around age sixty-five rather than working until they die. Even with all these recent developments, however, inherited wealth is still a significant source of funds for many American families. Experts estimate that around 80 percent of household wealth has been inherited, and the average American who died in 2015 left approximately $177,000 to his or her heirs.[119]

Inheritance laws in England were originally written to protect the wealth of powerful families and pass land and titles intact to the next generation.

Origin of Inheritance Laws

English inheritance laws originally developed to meet the needs of kings and lords rather than ordinary citizens. English laws of succession evolved to favor wealthy landed families by passing real estate and family titles to the eldest surviving son to keep wealth and power in the same family for generations. Younger sons and daughters were gifted money from the family's personal property and were expected to marry well or enter the military or clergy to earn a living.

In contrast, the American colonies developed a democratic system of inheritance where land was generally divided equally among all the sons—and occasionally bequeathed to daughters as well. This egalitarian system fit the needs of democratic Americans because land was plentiful and few families owned vast plantations. A small number of southern families, who owned large tracts of land and used slave labor to grow cotton and tobacco, passed laws favoring inheritance of the family land by the oldest surviving son, but these laws were rare in America and were abolished after the Civil War.

The laws of intestate succession control who takes property when a person dies without leaving a will.

Intestate Succession

When someone dies without a will, the estate code where he or she lived determines who inherits the assets. How property is distributed after a person dies without a will depends on whether he or she was married, whether the property was characterized as community or separate, whether assets are real estate or personal property, whether the decedent was single or widowed, and whether he or she left surviving children. Estate codes try to be fair, but they treat all families the same, so intestate succession is not always a good substitute for a basic estate plan.

The Basic Estate Plan

The elements of an estate plan include a will, power of attorney, medical power of attorney, directive to physicians, a HIPAA release, and occasionally a living trust to avoid the expense and publicity of probate or to care for minor or disabled children who need guidance and support. A will controls how assets are distributed, a power of attorney grants another person authority to act if you are unable to handle your own affairs, a medical power of attorney gives another person authority to make healthcare decisions for you when you can't make those decisions yourself, a directive to physicians communicates your wishes about end-of-life care, and a HIPAA release is an authorization to disclose protected health information to listed individuals. A living trust avoids probate and a trustee can manage and distribute assets to a widow, minors, or disabled children according to the terms of the trust document.

Early laws of inheritance were concerned primarily with keeping land within the family.

Early Inheritance Laws

Important goals of early inheritance laws were keeping ancestral lands in the family and determining who would take the land when a father died. The basic elements of inheritance law were developed in Mesopotamia during the reign of King Hammurabi. These inheritance laws were borrowed, modified, and extended by the Greeks, Romans, French, and English. American laws of succession followed English common law during the colonial period and then developed variations more suited to America's social and economic needs after the colonies won their independence from Britain.

Babylonian society contained three broad social classes, with a king above everyone and exempt from his own laws. King John, who was forced to sign the English Magna Carta on June 15, 1215, was the first monarch to accept restrictions on his absolute power to make and enforce laws. The Code of Hammurabi applied to all social classes and contained provisions for guardianship, rights of widows to a dowry that was inherited by her children, the rights of sons to inherit from their father, the status of illegitimate children, and protections for widows and daughters. The code also provided for the care of minor children, allowed a husband to gift property to his wife and daughters during his lifetime, prohibited fathers from disinheriting sons without good cause, and allowed illegitimate children who were acknowledged by their father to inherit a portion of his assets when he died.

The Greeks borrowed from the Code of Hammurabi and developed the written will to control the inheritance of property if there was no surviving son.

Greek Inheritance Laws.[120]

The Greeks developed written wills to control the distribution of assets, but a Greek last will became effective only if the father left no surviving son. A surviving son automatically took his father's land according to Greek law. Any legitimate male citizen over twenty years of age could draft a will in ancient Greece. In Athens, if a man had only daughters, he could leave his estate to an unrelated male who was obligated to marry one of the dead father's daughters if he wanted to keep the inheritance. Greek law required a will be attested by several witnesses. Greek estates were divided equally among the surviving sons, so individual family landholdings grew smaller over generations. Aristotle discussed the problems created by dividing land among several sons and said the practice often produced poverty and conflict.

Ancient Romans borrowed heavily from Greek laws of inheritance and developed them in important ways we follow even today.

Roman Inheritance Laws

Roman Laws were organized and published in the Twelve Tables during the fifth century BC.[121] The Twelve Tables included laws governing contracts, civil procedure, family law, criminal law, and rules of inheritance. They stated that if a father died without a will and left no heir, his nearest descendant from the same male ancestor would become his heir. They also stated that if the son was a minor, the nearest male heir would act as his guardian until the son reached adulthood. Romans borrowed wills from the Greeks and formalized their drafting and validation. Early Roman wills had to be announced before seven witnesses and could not be changed once they were signed and attested. A new will was needed if the testator changed his or her mind about the disposition of assets. Roman wills were first made by legionnaires on the eve of battle and were usually oral, but later Roman wills were written because testators didn't trust witness memories.

Roman citizens who had no sons often adopted a relative to receive their assets. For example, Julius Caesar named Octavius as his adopted son and heir to his fortune and the throne of Rome. Ancient Roman wills could not be contested if a child received a legacy, no matter how small, because the bequest showed the testator had considered the heir and given him or her a proper gift. A Roman testator had to be competent, the will had to be attested by seven witnesses, and the citizen had to leave some of his property to his widow and children. Ancient Roman wills were opened and validated through a formal procedure that evolved into modern probate law—attesting witnesses attended the opening of the will and verified that it was genuine, unchanged, and their seals had not been broken prior to the opening.

Jewish laws of inheritance developed rules similar to Roman law, but they were based primarily on the Bible and Jewish religious traditions.

Jewish Inheritance Law.[122]

Jewish families were encouraged to bequeath a portion of their estate to the temple or synagogue when they died. Jewish inheritance laws were designed to keep ancestral land in the family if possible. A Jewish family could sell land at a below-market price and redeem it later for the same price if it experienced financial distress. Jewish firstborn sons generally received a double share of their father's property according to biblical tradition, and younger sons took a single share. Illegitimate Jewish sons could not inherit from their father, and Jewish daughters were provided a dowry rather than land when they married. If a Jewish father had no sons, his eldest daughter inherited the family land, but she had to marry within her father's clan to keep the property. Gifting of land while the father lived was allowed to avoid the rigid rules of intestate succession. Gifting was a bilateral transaction that required acceptance, while inheritance was unilateral and could not be refused.

After the French Revolution, Napoleon modernized French laws of succession to make them uniform and fair.

The Napoleonic Code.[123]

Napoleon's famous code forbade a father disinheriting his children but allowed him to bequeath half his estate by gift or will if one child survived, or a third of the estate if two or more children survived. The code was designed to keep ancestral lands in the father's family, so inheritance laws made it difficult to leave land to a widow. French marriages were generally arranged, and the marriage contract was provided for the widow in case of her husband's death. An illegitimate child could not inherit from his father unless legally recognized according to the Napoleonic Code. Not until 1972 did French inheritance law allow illegitimate children to share equally in their parent's estate.

Early English common law borrowed heavily from Roman and Norman laws of inheritance.

English Inheritance Laws

Anglo-Saxon succession prior to the Norman Conquest followed early Germanic traditions, Christian canon law, and Roman inheritance rules.[124] Inheritance of the English throne varied between Germanic and Roman Catholic traditions. Teutonic customs allowed a king to choose his successor from among several candidates, whereas within the Christian tradition, the eldest son had the strongest claim to his father's throne because Christians believed God made their kings.

Anglo-Saxons divided land among the owner's sons, with the firstborn often having the right to select the best land and take his father's titles. When a Saxon died without a will, his lands were divided justly among his wife, children, and near kinsmen. If there were no sons, daughters could inherit land, but that was rare.

Anglo-Saxon nobility was divided into social classes with a king on top. Just below the king were ealdorman, similar to dukes, earls, and bishops in later English history. Titles were distributed by the king for service in war. Below the ealdorman were shire-reeves, who collected taxes and kept order. At the bottom of the ruling classes were thanes, equivalent to medieval knights who owned land and fought for the king when called to arms. Anglo-Saxon women gained some independence as they moved from being single to marriage and then to widowhood, but they enjoyed few legal rights. Anglo-Saxon nobles could devise these lands by will, and the use of wills was supported by the Catholic Church because many Anglo-Saxons gifted land to the Church when they died.

After the Norman Conquest, the doctrine of feudal tenure fundamentally changed the inheritance of land in England.

Norman Inheritance Laws.[125]

King William made major changes in the laws of inheritance for upper-class Normans after the conquest because he was concerned about Anglo-Saxon revolts. William established a feudal system of land ownership to ensure his followers owned allegiance to their king and held sufficient land to support a standing army of knights to suppress any uprising. Under the feudal system, the oldest surviving son inherited his father's title and real estate to ensure feudal knights had sufficient wealth to maintain a large armed force to fight for the king when needed.

The Norman feudal system resulted in the English doctrine of primogeniture—the right of succession to all a father's land and title by his firstborn son. In England, daughters were given dowries and married off to sons of other aristocratic families, establishing social, financial, and political connections, whereas younger sons were sent into the army or clergy to earn a living. Primogeniture lasted until 1925, when the Settled Land Act was passed by Parliament.

Ancient Anglo-Saxons didn't need a will to pass personal property; by custom, a widow inherited half her husband's personal property if he died leaving sons. However, the Catholic Church worked to make changes in inheritance laws to attract more bequeaths. As wills grew in importance, the rules for drafting a will became more formal. English wills had to be in writing, be notarized, be attested by the testator's seal, and bear the attesting seals of witnesses and an executor. With the passage of the Statute of Wills in 1540, Englishmen could dispose of nonfeudal land by wills enforced in civil courts. However, jurisdiction over wills disposing of personal property were handled by ecclesiastical courts. In 1670, another statute was passed by Parliament to control the inheritance of personal property when there was no will. Under this law, widows received one-third of all personal property owned by her husband, and their children inherited the remaining personal property in equal shares. If no children survived, the widow took half the personal property, and the husband's closest relatives received the other half.

In English inheritance law, the family bloodline was important, especially after the Norman Conquest, because feudal estates passed to the firstborn son. Primogeniture was never popular in colonial America except among a few Southern states, where families relied on slave labor to grow cotton and tobacco on large plantations. Family assets were generally distributed equally to the surviving spouse, sons, and daughters in America. A widow could receive between one-third and one-half the estate, and the children would inherit the balance in equal shares.

After wills became popular as a way to distribute land and personal property, English and American courts needed a systematic way to determine whether the document produced was the valid last will and testament of a deceased person. English and American courts borrowed early Roman practices to develop the modern probate system. Ancient Roman wills were sealed before being deposited in a safe place, usually the Senate, and were opened before a majority of the attesting witnesses after the testator died. The witnesses verified that the seals had not been broken, that the will carried their seals, and that it had not been altered.

Probate

The courts responsible for authenticating an English will changed after King William conquered England. He assigned jurisdiction over the inheritance of personal property to ecclesiastical courts, whereas jurisdiction over succession to freehold real estate was given to common-law civil courts. Feudal land passed automatically to the eldest surviving son. Because English creditors could sue in common-law courts and receive a judgment against the decedent's personal property for debts owed, this practice created conflicts between church and civil courts. To resolve these conflicts, the king established chancery courts, which decided cases when the king believed that common-law court decisions were rigid and unfair.

Chancery Courts

Conflicting claims to land or personal property were assigned to the chancery courts for settlement. However, a chancery court had to wait until an ecclesiastical court issued letters of administration and validated the will before it could hear the case. In England, ecclesiastical courts gradually lost jurisdiction over wills governing the inheritance of personal property, although they retained their power over issuing letters testamentary to executors into the nineteenth century.

American colonists brought the English common law with them, but primogeniture never developed in New England. A few Southern colonies developed a system of succession that kept large plantations in the same family for generations.[126]

American Probate Courts

American colonies never established ecclesiastical courts, so probate procedures were vested in secular civil courts even before the American Revolution. American civil procedures allowed the adjudication of wills dealing with land and personal property in the same civil court, unlike in England. The probate process was initiated by an executor filing the original will for probate. If an executor neglected to file the original will with the probate court, an interested party such as a beneficiary could file the will instead. A probate court determines whether the will was properly executed and issues letters testamentary to the executor so he or she can administer the estate. If there is a will contest, the probate court will determine whether the testator had capacity and whether there was undue influence or fraud involved in the making of the will.

Any interested party may contest a will by alleging a defect in its execution, a lack of capacity, fraud, or undue influence.

Will Contests.[127]

Experts estimate that about 1 percent of wills are disputed in America. Claiming a will was not properly executed is rarely successful because courts are reluctant to throw out a will based on a minor drafting error. Generally, a person contesting a will claims the testator lacked capacity or was subject to undue influence, or that the will was fraudulently induced. The person contesting a will must show he or she has standing (meaning the person will be damaged if the will is valid), state the alleged defect in the will, and prove it in court. Lack of capacity is usually shown by testimony from persons who knew the testator and a physician or psychologist who reviews medical records and offers an expert opinion about the competence of the testator. A person lacks capacity if he is a minor, demented, or insane and cannot recall his assets, his relatives, and the relationship between his assets and relatives.

Undue influence is usually proved by showing someone had the opportunity to pressure the testator, the testator was subject to undue influence, the will is different from what would normally be expected, and it appears to be the result of undue influence. Revocation of a will can be shown by evidence that the testator intended to revoke his will, especially if the original will can't be found. Forgery is an uncommon claim, although some lawyers have tried to defraud beneficiaries by drafting a will after the client died. Undue influence and lack of capacity are the most common allegations in will contests.

Trusts have become a significant part of modern estate planning.

Origin of Trusts.[128]

Trusts were developed by courts of equity to avoid the rigid rules of English common law governing legal title and use of real property. Trust doctrines developed when judges decided cases on the basis of fairness rather than the common law. Equity court judges enforced informal agreements between a manager or trustee who held legal title to land and an owner or beneficiary who asked the trustee to hold the land for his use and return it at a later date. These arrangements became a problem when some trustees decided not to honor their agreements to return the land to its rightful owner—such as when a knight returned from the crusades or when land gifted to the Church was transferred to a trustee for use by the Church. Common-law courts could not hear evidence about informal agreements and would not separate legal title from equitable use of land, so trustees were unfairly keeping land entrusted to them.

Rather than allow a manager or trustee to claim title to the land fraudulently, equitable courts enforced the informal agreements between a crusader or the Church and the trustee. Equity courts forced the trustee or manager to return the land to its rightful owner. English common law was no help because it regarded rights to land as indivisible, so when law courts were confronted with a case where a trustee held legal title to the land, the common-law courts would not hear evidence of a prior agreement between the trustee and the settlor. Because a common-law court could not recognize the separation of legal title and equitable use of land, it could not give the rightful owner a remedy.

English kings deemed it unfair to allow their knights to be defrauded by dishonest trustees, so they established equity courts with flexible rules to hear these cases. Equity courts ruled that legal title to land could be separated from equitable enjoyment of the land, thus establishing the concept of land held in trust for the use of another.

Trust law borrowed the concept of fiduciary duty from ancient contract law.

Fiduciary Duty

The law of trusts was gradually developed by equity courts and allowed a person, called a settlor, to transfer legal title to a trustee who was obligated to hold, administer, and distribute the property to named beneficiaries under the terms of the trust instrument. Courts of equity applied the idea of a fiduciary duty (a legal concept developed to enforce contracts between merchants and their agents) owed by a trustee to the beneficiary. Early fiduciary laws were used to enforce duties owed by an agent to a merchant who gave him funds to purchase goods in another city and have them delivered to the merchant's base of operations.

The duties of a fiduciary include loyalty, care, and prudence. The idea of fiduciary duty and its enforcement was so important that four chapters of the English Magna Charta listed remedies for heirs against guardians who breached their fiduciary duties by withholding or wasting the ward's inheritance. Current fiduciary duties in English and American law exceed those developed earlier, but the beginnings of a trustee's fiduciary duties are clearly visible as early at the thirteenth century in England. Moreover, the enforcement of fiduciary duties led to the development of two types of trusts in England, active and passive trusts.

Trusts were also developed to circumvent the restrictions Norman feudal tenure placed on the ownership and conveyance of land.

Large tracts of land in England were held under feudal tenure, and the king was entitled to a payment when land descended from a father to his eldest surviving son, when a wardship was established because the inheritor was a minor, on the marriage of a daughter of the lord, on the knighting of his eldest son, or when a lord was captured and held for ransom during war. By establishing a trust and giving legal title to another, the landholder or settlor hoped to escape many of these feudal burdens and gain the right to transfer land outside his immediate family or gift the land by will at his death to someone other than his eldest son.

Another motive for the development of trusts was that English law forbade religious corporations from owning land because the king could not collect taxes from the church. By using a trust, religious orders were able to enjoy the benefits of holding land without breaking the law by holding legal title to land themselves. The Church assigned legal title to a trustee, and he paid taxes to the king while the church managed the land and enjoyed its income and benefits.

American Trust Law

Today, it's possible to create trusts that are effective during the lifetime of the settlor (living trusts) as well as trusts that become effective at death (testamentary trusts). The settlor usually appoints himself or herself trustee to manage and administer a living trust during the settlor's lifetime and then names a successor trustee to hold the trust property for successor beneficiaries after the settlor's death. The trustee has a fiduciary duty to carry out the terms of the trust without self-interest. The trustee must manage, invest, and distribute the trust property according to the terms of the trust, and if he or she does not, the trustee is in breach of his or her fiduciary duty and can be liable for damages and removal.

Business Trusts

Special trusts were used in the nineteenth and early twentieth century to control the manufacturing and distribution of kerosene and steel, the mining and distribution of diamonds, producing and marketing cigarettes, and transatlantic shipping, among other business enterprises.

These giant business trusts accumulated monopoly pricing power and eventually were dissolved by the US government through antitrust suits. Congress passed the Sherman Antitrust Act, the graduated income tax, and the estate tax to break up monopoly trusts, tax wealthy individuals, redistribute funds to the poor, and prevent wealthy families from passing large fortunes to their children when they died.

A permanent estate tax was passed in 1916 to raise money and limit financial inequality in America.

Death and Taxes.[129]

When a person dies, the estate may be liable for a tax on all assets owned—money in the bank, houses, stocks, bonds, and commodities. Estate taxes were introduced during the American Civil War and again in 1898 to meet extraordinary government expenses, but these earlier estate taxes were repealed when the crises were over. In contrast, the current estate tax has never been repealed. The original version of the estate tax exempted the first $50,000 from tax, and the top tax rate was 10 percent on assets over $1 million. In the beginning, estate taxes fell only on a few wealthy families, but as time passed, inflation increased the value of assets, estate tax rates became more progressive, and the nominal value of exemptions fell, so more families owed estate taxes. In the 1930s, only about 1 percent of American families paid an estate tax. By the 1970s, over 7 percent of families paid estate taxes, and the rates were much higher than in the 1930s.

To reverse this trend, President Ronald Reagan raised exemptions and lowered estate tax rates in the 1980s. The estate tax exemption in 2020 was $11.58 million per individual, which means that very few families pay estate taxes today. Wealthy families could also avoid estate taxes by gifting large sums to family members prior to death or establishing trusts for their grandchildren. To stop this avoidance of estate taxes, gift and generation skipping tax laws were passed. Recently, several states have repealed estate tax laws to attract wealthy families. The repealing of state estate tax laws was initiated in Florida, New Mexico, and Texas to attract wealthy individuals from high-tax states such as California and New York. Later, the estate tax was abolished by referendum in California because voters believed that small farmers and business owners would be forced to sell their land or companies when they died to pay estate taxes.

Another significant trend in America is the growing power of women over their own property, including the right to control land and other assets inherited from their family of origin. Women have gained essentially equal footing with men in the ownership of property, and they draft half of all wills in America today.

ENDNOTES

1. *Texas Estate Code*, Title 2 E. Intestate Succession, 2019.
2. Editorial Team, "Average Inheritance: How Much Are Retirees Leaving to Heirs?" *New Retirement*, 2017.
3. "Primogeniture," *Merriam-Webster Unabridged Dictionary*, 2014.
4. Lee J. Alston and Morton O. Schapiro, "Inheritance Laws across Colonies: Causes and Consequences," *Journal of Economic History* 44, no. 2 (1984): 277–87.
5. Henry C. Black, *Black's Law Dictionary*, 6th ed. (St. Paul, MN: West, 1990).
6. Ibid.
7. Ibid.
8. *Texas Estate Code*, Title 2 E. Intestate Succession, 2019.
9. Julia Kagan, "Estate Planning," Investopedia, 2019.
10. Ben Geier, "What Is the Lifetime Gift Tax Exemption?" *Asset* (2019).
11. John Simkin, "The Norman Feudal System," *Spartacus Educational* (2016).
12. Lee J. Alston and Morton O. Schapiro, "Inheritance Laws across Colonies: Causes and Consequences."
13. History.com, "Code of Hammurabi," History.com, 2019.
14. Nigel G. Wilson, "Ancient Greek Wills—Inheritance," *Encyclopedia of Ancient Greece* (New York: Routledge, 2006), 380–82.
15. Fordham Editors, "Ancient History Sourcebook: The Law Code of Gortyn (Crete), c. 450 B.C.E.," *Ancient History Sourcebook* (2020).
16. Lin Foxhall, *Female Inheritance in Athenian Law* (Center for Hellenic Studies, Harvard University).
17. Probability/Statistics in Inheritance. 9/14/2005 https://www.lehigh.ecu/-jas0/G08.htm/
18. Mark Cartwright, "Twelve Tables," *Ancient History Encyclopedia* (2016).
19. Rafael Domingo, *The Roman Law of Succession. An Overview* (2017).

20 Bruce Wells, *Inheritance Laws in Ancient Israel*, Bible Odyssey, 2020.
21 Jonathan S. Milgram, *From Mesopotamia to the Mishnah. Tannaitic Inheritance Law in Its Legal and Social Contexts* (Brighton, MA: Academic Studies, 2019), 66–75.
22 Cemal Kutay Koman, *The Napoleonic Code* Guided History, Boston University.
23 Benoit Duchan, "Everything You Need to Know Before Making a French Will," *Complete France*, 2017.
24 A. H. F. Lefroy, "The Anglo-Saxon Period of English Law," *Yale Law Journal* 26, no. 4 (1917): 291–303.
25 Anglo-Saxon England—Structure of Society, Google site.
26 Dorothy Whitelock, ed., *Anglo-Saxon Wills* (London: Cambridge University Press, 1930).
27 History on the Net, "Medieval Life-Feudalism and the Feudal System," Salem Media, 2020.
28 "Entail," *Cambridge Academic Content Dictionary*.
29 Elizabeth P. Pauls, "Primogeniture and Ultimageniture," *Encyclopaedia Britannica*.
30 University of Nottingham Manuscripts and Special Collections, *Common Recovery*, University of Nottingham.
31 University of Nottingham Manuscripts and Special Collections, *Strict Settlement Agreement*, University of Nottingham.
32 UK Public General Acts, *Settled Land Act 1925*, Legislationgov.UK, 1925.
33 "What Are the Requirements of a Valid Will?" HG.org.
34 "Ecclesiastical Court," *Encyclopaedia Britannica*.
35 "Statute of Wills," *Encyclopaedia Britannica*.
36 "What Is the Statute of Frauds?" HG.org.
37 Salmon, Marylynn, *The Legal Status of Women, 1776–1830*, The Gilder Lehrman Institute of American History Advanced Placement United States History Guide, 1998.
38 Carole Shammas, Marylynn Salmon, and Michel Dahlin, *Inheritance in America* (Galveston, TX: Frontier, 1997), 41–62.
39 Ibid.
40 Lee J. Alston and Morton O. Schapiro, "Inheritance Laws across Colonies: Causes and Consequences," Journal of Economic History 44, no. 2 (1984): 277–87.
41 Dominik Lasok, "Virginia Bastardy Laws: A Burdensome Heritage," *William and Mary Law Review* 9 (1967): 402–29.
42 "Marital Property: Who Owns What?" FindLaw.com.
43 "Texas Homestead Law Overview," FindLaw.com.

44 "An American Time Capsule: Three Centuries of Broadsides and Other Printed Ephemera—Women and Reform," LibraryofCongress.gov.
45 Julia Kagan, "Social Security," Investopedia, 2019. Julia Kagan, "Estate Tax," Investopedia, 2019.
46 "What's Medicare?" Medicare.gov, 2020.
47 Lake, Rebecca, "How a Bypass Trust Works in an Estate Plan," Smart Asset, 2020.
48 Julie Garber, "What Happens during the Probate Process?" The Balance, 2019.
49 Randolph Richards, "A Scroll with Seven Seals," Randolphrichards.com, 2016.
50 Eugene A. Haertle, "The History of the Probate Court," *Marquette Law Review* 45 (1962): 546–50.
51 Ibid.
52 Ibid.
53 "Statute of Wills," Encyclopedia.com., 2019.
54 "Court of Probate Act 1857," *World Heritage Encyclopedia.*
55 "State Probate Courts," FindLaw.com, 2019.
56 ABA, "The Probate Process," ABA Estate Planning FAQs.
57 Rania Combs, "Why Should My Will Include a Self-Proving Affidavit?" Raniacomb.com, 2018.
58 Rania Combs, "Is It Possible to Probate a Lost Will?" Raniacombs.com, 2012.
59 Robert Ray, "Step by Step Guide to Contest a Will in Texas," Texas Inheritance, 2014.
60 Ibid.
61 Ibid.
62 Mary Joy Quinn, "Defining Undue Influence," ABA.com, 2018.
63 Jose Rivera, "Testamentary Capacity in Drafting a Will," Legal Match.
64 "Probate Fraud and Will Forgery," DAS Law, 2018.
65 "Breach of Fiduciary Duty Law and Legal Definition," US Legal, 2019.
66 David J. Seipp, "Trust and Fiduciary Duty in the Early Common Law," *Boston University Law Review* 91 (2002): 1011–39.
67 Ibid.
68 Ibid.
69 Martin M. Shenkman, *The Modern Revocable Trust* (Estate Planning Studies, 2016).
70 "Mortmain," Britannica.com.
71 David J. Seipp, "Trust and Fiduciary Duty in the Early Common Law," *Boston University Law Review* 91 (2002): 1011–39.

72 Ibid.
73 Brian Duignan, "Chancery Division," *Encyclopaedia Britannica*.
74 Ibid.
75 William Hamilton Bryson, *Cases Concerning Equity and the Courts of Equity—1550–1660* (Richmond School of Law-Law Faculty Publications, 2001).
76 David J. Seipp, "Trust and Fiduciary Duty in the Early Common Law," *Boston University Law Review* 91 (2002): 1011–39.
77 "Breach of Fiduciary Duty Law and Legal Definition," US Legal, 2019.
78 "Code of Hammurabi," History.com, 2019.
79 Vincent R. Johnson, "The Fiduciary Obligations of Public Officials," *St. Mary's Journal on Legal Malpractice and Ethics* (2019): 298.
80 *Meinhard v. Salmon*, 249 NY 458, 1928.
81 David J. Seipp, "Trust and Fiduciary Duty in the Early Common Law," *Boston University Law Review* 91 (2002): 1011–39.
82 Julia Kagan, "Active Trust," Investopedia, 2018.
83 David T. Smith, "The Statute of Uses: A Look at Its Historical Evolution and Demise," *Case Western Reserve Law Review* 18 (1966): 40.
84 "Statute of Uses," FreeDictionary.com.
85 David J. Seipp, "Trust and Fiduciary Duty in the Early Common Law," *Boston University Law Review* 91 (2002): 1011–39.
86 "Alexander the Great's Will Found 2,000 Years After Death," Daily Mail Online.
87 "Gaius Julius Caesar: Inheritance," Livius.org, 2009.
88 "Revision of Last Will and Testament: Henry VIII," TudorsDynasty.com, 2016.
89 "William Shakespeare's Last Will and Testament: Original Copy Including Three Signatures." Shakespeare Documented, National Archives, UK.
90 "George Washington's Last Will and Testament, 9 July 1799," Founders Online, 2002.
91 "Last Will and Testament of Napoleon," The Dearly Departed, 2012.
92 "Thomas Jefferson: Will and Codicil, 16–17 Mar. 1826, 16 March 1826," 2002.
93 "Last Will and Testament of Robert E. Lee, 1846," UShistory.org.
94 Julie Garber, "Celebrities Who Died without a Will—Abraham Lincoln," The Balance, 2019.
95 "The Last Will of Queen Victoria," Royal Central, 2019.
96 "Franklin D. Roosevelt, Original Carbon Copy of His Complete Last Will and Testament, December 14, 1941," Heritage Auctions.

97 "John F. Kennedy's Last Will and Testament," Brannigan and Murphy, 2018.
98 "Last Will and Testament of Winston Churchill, January 24, 1965," 2019.
99 Frank J. Prial, "Accord Reached on Johnson Will," New York Times, June 3, 1986.
100 "Settlement Ends Dallas Legal Feud between H. L. Hunt Heirs," *Dallas Morning News*, May 6, 2010.
101 John Eligon, "Settlement in Battle over Astor Estate Is Reached," *New York Times*, March 28, 2012.
102 Daniel Schulman, "Koch vs. Koch: The Brutal Battle That Tore Apart America's Most Powerful Family," Mother Jones, May 20, 2014.
103 Ronald Colicchio, "Lessons from the Leona Helmsley Estate," The Probate Litigation Resource Center, June 9, 2015.
104 Daniel Fisher, "Court Ruling Likely Ends Anna Nichole Smith Estate's Fight for Marshall Family Millions," *Forbes*, July 14, 2015.
105 *Stern vs. Marshall*, 564 U.S. 462, 2011.
106 Scott Johnson, "B. B. King's Estate War: 15 Kids, 15 Moms and a 'Totally Haywire' Fight," *Hollywood Reporter*, May 26, 2016.
107 Meg James, "Sumner Redstone and Family Settle Legal Dispute with His Ex-Companion Manuela Herzer," *Los Angeles Times*, January 8, 2019.
108 Matthew Josephson, "The Origin of the Trusts," Panarchy, 1934.
109 The Sherman Antitrust Act of 1890, 15 U.S.C. 1-7.
110 Troy Segal, "Clayton Antitrust Act," Investopedia, 2019.
111 Standard Oil Trust, "United States History."
112 Ron Chernow, "The Deal of the Century," *American Heritage* 49 (1998).
113 "Tobacco Trust," Encyclopedia.com.
114 Paul Zimnisky, "A Brief History of De Beers," Diamond Analytics, 2019.
115 Gabriel Bowers, "The International Mercantile Marine Company," in R. Rick Spilman, "J. P. Morgan, RMS *Titanic* and SS United States," Old Salt Blog, 2012.
116 Archibald MacLeish, "The Grand Scheme of the Swedish Match King," *Fortune*, 2009.
117 "Uniform International Wills Act Law and Legal Definition," USLegal.com.
118 Julia Kagan, "Payable on Death (POD)," Investopedia, 2019.
119 "Average Inheritance: How Much Are Retirees Leaving to Heirs?" New Retirement, 2017.
120 Nigel G. Wilson, "Ancient Greek Wills—Inheritance," *Encyclopedia of Ancient Greece* (New York, Routledge, 2006), 230–31.

121 *The Twelve Tables*, Yale Law School Lillian Goldman Law Library, The Avalon Project.
122 Jonathan S. Milgram, *From Mesopotamia to the Mishnah. Tannaitic Inheritance Law in Its Legal and Social Contexts*, (Brighton, MA: Academic Studies Press, 2019), 66–75.
123 Cemal Kutay Koman, "The Napoleonic Code," Guided History, Boston University.
124 A. H. F. Lefroy, "The Anglo-Saxon Period of English Law," *Yale Law Journal* 26, no. 4 (1917): 291–303.
125 John Simkin, "The Norman Feudal System," Spartacus Educational, 2016.
126 Lee J. Alston and Morton O. Schapiro, "Inheritance Laws across Colonies: Causes and Consequences," *Journal of Economic History* 44, no. 2 (1984): 277–87.
127 Wood Edwards, "How to Contest a Will in Texas," MyLawTeam.com.
128 "The Origins of Trusts and Fiduciary Duties," CSFME.com.
129 Gary Robbins, "Estate Taxes: An Historical Perspective," Heritage Foundation, 2004.

www.ingramcontent.com/pod-product-compliance
Lightning Source LLC
Chambersburg PA
CBHW032015170526
45157CB00002B/707